PRENTICE-HALL FOUNDATIONS OF PHILOSOPHY SERIES

Virgil Aldrich	Philosophy of Art
William Alston	Philosophy of Language
Stephen Barker	Philosophy of Mathematics
Roderick Chisholm	Theory of Knowledge
William Dray	Philosophy of History
Joel Feinberg	Social Philosophy
William Frankena	Ethics
Martin Golding	Philosophy of Law
Carl Hempel	Philosophy of Natural Science
John Hick	Philosophy of Religion
David Hull	Philosophy of Biological Science
Willard Van Orman Quine	Philosophy of Logic
Richard Rudner	Philosophy of Social Science
Wesley Salmon	Logic
Jerome Shaffer	Philosophy of Mind
Richard Taylor	Metaphysics

Elizabeth and Monroe Beardsley, editors

PHILOSOPHY OF LAW

Martin P. Golding

DUKE UNIVERSITY

PRENTICE-HALL, INC.
Englewood Cliffs, New Jersey

Library of Congress Cataloging in Publication Data

GOLDING, MARTIN PHILIP, 1930—
  Philosophy of law.

  (Prentice-Hall foundations of philosophy series)
  Bibliography: p.
  1. Law—Philosophy. I. Title.
Law   340.1   74-12126
ISBN 0–13–664136–9
ISBN 0–13–664128–8 (pbk.)

To My Mother

© 1975 by
PRENTICE-HALL, INC.
Englewood Cliffs, New Jersey

10   9

PRENTICE-HALL INTERNATIONAL, INC., London
PRENTICE-HALL OF AUSTRALIA, PTY. LTD., Sydney
PRENTICE-HALL OF CANADA, LTD., Toronto
PRENTICE-HALL OF INDIA PRIVATE LIMITED, New Delhi
PRENTICE-HALL OF JAPAN, INC., Tokyo

FOUNDATIONS OF PHILOSOPHY

Many of the problems of philosophy are of such broad relevance to human concerns, and so complex in their ramifications, that they are, in one form or another, perennially present. Though in the course of time they yield in part to philosophical inquiry, they may need to be rethought by each age in the light of its broader scientific knowledge and deepened ethical and religious experience. Better solutions are found by more refined and rigorous methods. Thus, one who approaches the study of philosophy in the hope of understanding the best of what it affords will look for both fundamental issues and contemporary achievements.

Written by a group of distinguished philosophers, the Foundations of Philosophy Series aims to exhibit some of the main problems in the various fields of philosophy as they stand at the present stage of philosophical history.

While certain fields are likely to be represented in most introductory courses in philosophy, college classes differ widely in emphasis, in method of instruction, and in rate of progress. Every instructor needs freedom to change his course as his own philosophical interests, the size and makeup of his classes, and the needs of his students vary from year to year. The nineteen volumes in the Foundations of Philosophy Series—each complete in itself, but complementing the others—offer a new flexibility to the instructor, who can create his own textbook by combining several volumes as he wishes, and can choose different combinations at different times. Those volumes that are not used in an introductory course will be found valuable, along with other texts or collections of readings, for the more specialized upper-level courses.

Elizabeth Beardsley / *Monroe Beardsley*

10.95

v

CONTENTS

PREFACE

The field of legal philosophy, which, with a few notable exceptions, was recently cultivated mainly within the technical confines of the law school or as a sub-branch of ethics and political philosophy, has experienced a considerable enlivening in the past two decades in the English-speaking world. Aside from the appearance of important books and articles, there has been an expansion of course offerings in the philosophy of law on both the undergraduate and graduate levels and also an enriching of the "jurisprudence" syllabus in law schools. I hope, with this little book, to contribute toward these trends.

My work on this book was well under way, only to be interrupted by the events that shook the academic world, especially Columbia University, in 1968. It was some time before I was able to turn my mind back to sustained scholarly work and bring my task to completion. It is possible that this book would have been rather different had it been produced sooner. Whether the longer gestation period improved the result, I do not have the psychological distance to judge. At any rate, I am more than ever convinced of the intellectual and practical significance of the subject.

My aim has been to introduce the student to legal philosophy and to stimulate his own thinking. Naturally, I would be gratified if the expert in the field also finds a few novelties here and there. One of the problems I faced was the selection of topics for coverage. I am not entirely confident that my solution was correct or that the proper balance was finally given to the matters herein considered. Many subjects had to be excised because of the limitation of space. The most difficult task, however, was that of compression, but I trust that clarity did not suffer too much in the process. I also regret that I was unable to take account of a number of important works (some are cited in the bibliography) which appeared in the course of the writing.

Parts of Chapter 3 first appeared in my article, "Private Right and the Limits of Law," *Philosophy East and West,* 21 (1971), 375–88, and I thank the editor and the University of Hawaii Press for permission to reprint them here. I also took up the subject of Chapter 6 first in an article, "Preliminaries to the Study of Procedural Justice," in Graham Hughes (ed.), *Law, Reason, and Justice* (1969), 71–100. This has now been considerably rewritten, but I wish to thank the editor and the New York University Press for permission to reprint whatever remains of the original.

My thanks go to Elizabeth and Monroe Beardsley, two angelic beings, for their patience and editorial advice. I also express my appreciation to my daughter Shulamith for her assistance with the proofreading. Special thanks go to my wife, whose help I cannot even begin to describe. Without her encouragement (and nagging), this book would still be undone.

M. P. G.

Introduction: The Scope of Legal Philosophy

The setting of Plato's dialogue *Crito* is the following: Socrates has been convicted of the crime of corrupting the youth of Athens by teaching an impious doctrine about the gods. For this, he has been sentenced to death by poison. He is now in prison awaiting the time at which he must drink the fatal cup. His friend and student Crito comes to visit him and explains that a "jailbreak" is all arranged. Crito offers various reasons as to why Socrates should escape. But is it right? asks Socrates. Is it right for someone who has been convicted of a crime—even if he believes his conviction was unjust—to avoid his punishment? More generally, is there an obligation to obey the law, and what can be the basis for such an obligation?

This dialogue illustrates the fact that the field of the philosophy of law overlaps other branches of philosophy. The *Crito* is not only one of the classics of legal philosophy; it is also one of the classics of ethics and political and social philosophy. The same holds for works by other writers—for instance, Hobbes' *Leviathan*. There are no sharp lines of demarcation to the philosophy of law. Certain problems are common to all these subjects, though they are often dealt with in legal philosophy

1

from a narrower perspective. This perspective also holds, and perhaps even more narrowly, for many works on "jurisprudence" which are devoted to explaining the basic doctrines and principles of a given legal system. These works are nevertheless of philosophical interest. Still, because of the ground they have in common, ethics and political and social philosophy have a great deal to learn from philosophical inquiry into law. The study of moral reasoning, for example, can be enriched by the study of legal reasoning.

The philosophy of law also shares another feature with the above-mentioned branches. It deals with two kinds of question: normative (or justificatory) and analytic (or conceptual). Plato's *Crito* provides an example of the first kind; it asks whether a certain act (or type of act) is right. His dialogue *Euthyphro* provides an example of a treatment of the second kind of question. In that dialogue Socrates engages Euthyphro in a discussion of the definition of "piety." Although some alleged instances of pious actions are mentioned, the interlocutors do not consider whether or not they really are pious. Instead, they are concerned with what piety is; they attempt to analyze the concept of piety, to explicate what the word means. Legal philosophers, too, answer questions about whether something is good, right, or just and also attempt to give analyses of concepts and definitions of various terms.

I shall now supply a very brief account of some of the main problems of legal philosophy. Not all of them will be taken up in this book, partly because of limitations of space and partly because they can be just as appropriately treated by works in other branches of philosophy. Some of them are discussed in other volumes in this series.

Perhaps the foremost of the problems of legal philosophy is the analysis of the concept of law. What is law? What does it mean to say that a legal system exists in a society? We shall devote the next chapter to identifying the issues of which this problem is comprised. In the second chapter various theories of the nature of law are given a critical exposition. One of the basic bones of contention is whether there is a necessary link between law and morality. Do the criteria for the existence of law also include a moral element? Can an unjust law be a valid law? These questions, important in their own right, also bear upon the analysis of the concept of legal obligation. Laws, typically, impose obligations to act or not act in a certain way. How shall legal obligation be understood: is it simply a question of force?

It is only a short step from this issue to the normative questions of whether, and under what conditions, there is a moral obligation to obey the law and whether disobedience is ever justified. Perhaps even more fundamental, however, is what justifies law in the first place. Why should a society have laws? This, of course, is not a question for the legal philosopher alone, but also for the political and social philosopher. It touches the very basic functions of politically organized community, many of which can be realized only through the instrumentality of law. In answering it, philosophers have invoked broad generalizations about human nature and social relationships. (Hobbes, for example, maintained that the state is necessary in order to curb innate human aggressiveness, and that laws provide the common standards of conduct without which social life would be impossible.) In this book we shall be concerned with the matters mentioned in this paragraph only to the extent that they are involved in the debate over the analysis of the concept of law.

Whether or not there is a necessary link between law and morality, it is a fact that we do pass judgment on the goodness or justness of laws. Newspaper editorials bombard us daily and Sunday with their judgments on some proposal in the legislative hopper. But what are the grounds for the evaluation of laws and, also, of the way they are administered? This is, ultimately, a normative question about the exercise of public power, and it is obviously not the exclusive province of the legal philosopher either, except insofar as he may be expected to bring to bear on it a closer attention to the actual operations and contents of legal systems. As one gets to evaluating particular laws, or even particular branches of law, it is clear that responsible evaluation presupposes social knowledge of an empirical kind, although there are difficult questions about how this knowledge is to be applied in the making of evaluations. The problem of evaluation also raises the more general one of what the aims of the law should be. Any concrete solution requires an examination of various interests, individual and social (e.g., security, economic welfare, etc.), and their critical assessment and ranking. In these connections, the legal philosopher will be concerned with problems of "institutional design," specifically with how legal institutions and agencies should be designed to achieve the aims of the law. There are numerous problems of this sort. We shall take up one of them, albeit on a theoretical level, in the last chapter.

If the philosophy of law is concerned with what the aims of law should be (and also, of course, with what the law can actually *do*), it must also concern itself with the permissible scope of the law, with its limits. Are there spheres of activity that are "not the law's business"? This is the ancient but ever new issue of authority and individual freedom, an issue which, to be sure, arises outside the legal context but which arises with particular sharpness for law, especially in the modern state. Can we formulate a principle that sets limits to the use of legal compulsion? The debate over this question is the subject of the third chapter of this book. The heart of the matter involves the protected rights that individuals should have.

The issue of standards for the critical evaluation of laws and legal institutions has an important place in the study of judicial decision making. Judges interpret and apply the law. They also make law. Anyone who has ever read a judicial opinion, which is intended as a justification of the decision in a case, will immediately see that the opinion represents a more or less elaborate reasoning process. But what are good reasons for a decision, and what makes an opinion well-reasoned? Complex matters of both a normative and analytical sort arise here. Judicial reasoning is like moral reasoning in many respects, yet it operates under the special constraints of the legal system and its aims. These likenesses and differences are topics for detailed investigation. Precedent, for example, might play a role in moral reasoning, but it certainly plays a role in judicial reasoning in most, perhaps all, systems. The idea of precedent is grist for the legal philosopher's analytical mill. Of equal significance are the normative questions of why, and to what extent, precedent ought to be followed. These large topics are not covered in this book, but the subject matter of the sixth chapter does have relevance to them.

The law employs many notable concepts in its formulation of legal rules and doctrines and in their further elaboration by judicial reasoning —for example, the concepts of property, persons, privacy, rights, duties, contract, and causation. One of the classic problems of the analytic side of legal philosophy, and one that is given extensive treatment in works on jurisprudence, concerns the extent to which certain of the concepts employed in law are reducible to others and how various concepts are logically or functionally related to others in judicial reasoning. Clearly, the analysis of at least some of the above concepts, and the justification of rules or doctrines that use them, are of interest to other branches of philosophy, too. Limitations of space preclude our taking up these topics in this book, although a little will be said about rights and privacy in Chapter Three.

Legal philosophy also overlaps a branch of philosophy which hitherto has not been mentioned—namely, philosophical psychology or philosophy of mind. Again, however, it treats its problems from a special point of view. These problems arise because various legal rules and doctrines employ concepts that have to do with modes of action and with mental states and events. For instance, in the civil law a person might be held liable for some damage which resulted from his negligent act; and in the criminal law the grade of an offense might depend on whether or not it was committed intentionally. So-called mental concepts are part and parcel of questions of the existence and extent of liability, civil and criminal, and the analysis of the notions of act, omission, motive, intention, etc. has been pursued with renewed vigor in recent years.

What should the basis of criminal liability be and when should someone be excused from punishment? This is the vexing issue of responsibility and the relationship that responsibility in the law should have to moral responsibility. Can we really distinguish between responsible and nonresponsible offenders, anyway? But it is not only important for the legal philosopher to examine the mental conditions that constitute grounds for an excuse; he must also inquire into why excuses should be allowed in the first place; for example, what is legal insanity, and should insanity be admitted as a defense? We shall not be able to go into the analysis of mental concepts in the law and the reasons for excuses. But we shall devote two chapters to the question of the justification of punishment. Why should we punish at all? The main answers will be critically examined.

Finally, there is the subject of justice. There are so many facets to this (e.g., political justice, economic justice, justice in commercial dealings, etc.) that I shall not attempt to describe them here. It is obvious that the subject of justice is not the private preserve of the legal philosopher, although justice is often regarded as the special virtue belonging to law. We shall only touch upon the question of the meaning of "just law" in a few places in this book. Justice in punishment, however, will occupy us considerably, and the last chapter is concerned with the role of procedural justice in the settlement of disputes.

But this is where we shall end and not where we start out. We shall begin with what I have called the foremost problem of legal philosophy, namely, the nature of law. Is it really true, as the young Alcibiades told the great Pericles, that no one really deserves praise unless he knows what a law is (Xenophon, *Memorabilia,* I, ii)? I doubt it, although there have been praiseworthy attempts to elucidate what law is.

CHAPTER ONE

The Nature
of Law:
Problems

In this chapter we will be concerned with one of the central problems of legal philosophy, namely, the nature of law. Our interest will be focused, in particular, on delineating the issues that surround this topic rather than upon theories that have been developed in attempting to handle them. It is only after the issues have been exposed to view that we shall be in a position both to understand the arguments for the theories and to evaluate their adequacy.

The question "What is law?" has had a long history and many answers have been given to it. Many of these, however, are not alternative answers to the same question, but answers to different questions about the nature of law.[1] This is hardly surprising, for law is a complex phenomenon whose elements may be examined from a variety of perspectives and interests. In this respect, the history of the analysis of the nature of law is not unlike that of other fields of philosophical inquiry in which complex phenomena (e.g., science, history, and art) are analyzed. Our task in this chapter is, in effect, to break down this question into a set of questions which formulate the issues inherent in the problem of the nature

[1] See Richard Wollheim, "The Nature of Law," *Political Studies,* 2 (1954), 128–44.

of law. I shall shortly develop a heuristic device that will enable us to do this in a systematic way.

THE DEFINITION OF "LAW"

In asking "What is law?"—whatever the complexities this question contains or conceals—the philosopher is most of all seeking to define "law" or analyze the concept of law. In traditional terms, he would be said to be seeking the *essence* of law. What this means may be understood by considering a classical example for purposes of illustration: the nature of man. In asking what the nature of man is, we are seeking those qualities that are necessarily shared by all humans. According to an ancient view (whose correctness is of no concern to us), these are rationality and animality. We may think of these qualities as elements that make up the notion of humanity. Alternatively, we may say that the term "human" is synonymous with the phrase "rational animal." Whichever way we choose to look at the matter, according to this view a statement of the form

X is human

(e.g., "John is human") is true if, and only if, the conjunction of statements of the following forms is true:

i] X is rational.
ii] X is an animal.

These two statement-forms give the set of necessary and sufficient conditions for the truth of a statement of the form "X is human." This is equivalent to saying that rationality and animality are the "essence" of humanity.

Analogously to this illustration, the attempt to define "law" or analyze the concept of law, in the sense of specifying its essence, is a search for the set of qualities that are necessary and sufficient to characterize law. That is to say, there is some form of statement containing the word "law," or some closely related term such as "legal," for which we wish to specify the set of statements each of which is necessary for its truth and which together are jointly sufficient for its truth. Now, in undertaking such an inquiry, it is useful to select for initial examination a form of statement which provides a fruitful focus of attention and which helps us to uncover the various ramifications of the problem of the nature of law. The form we shall consider is

A legal system exists in S

where S refers to any given society. In attempting to supply the necessary and sufficient conditions for assertions of this form, we shall be able to uncover, in an orderly manner, the complex of questions that are implicit in asking "What is law?" They are offshoots of a central theme.

The word "law" is, of course, used in a variety of contexts. It is used, for example, to refer to *a* law (a rule of law) and to *the* law (the laws that prevail in a given society). The explication of such uses is an important part of the problem of the nature of law, and this task arises as a special topic under the approach we are adopting. But "law" is also used to refer to a certain kind of social institution, and it is this rich use to which statements of the form "A legal system exists in *S*" are particularly related. We shall, in effect, be attempting to elucidate what is meant in saying that *a legal system exists in a society* or (to put it in other words) to analyze the concept of the existence of a legal system. If we can supply the necessary and sufficient conditions for the truth of statements of the selected form, we shall have come pretty close, at least, to specifying the essence of law. It should be kept in mind, however, that our primary aim in this chapter is to delineate the issues rather than the solutions to the problem.

It is important here to take note of a potential difficulty. It may well be the case that there is *no* essence of a legal system in the sense of a single set (or, more exactly, a single schema) of individually necessary and jointly sufficient conditions for the truth of "A legal system exists in *S*." There may instead be several different, though overlapping, sets of sufficient conditions. In other words, there may be more than one way for something to qualify as a legal system. Moreover, as has been argued, the existence of a legal system may be a matter of degree, and there may also be borderline cases of legal systems. Some legal theorists have made even stronger claims than any of these. Given the many controversies over the nature of law, these writers have apparently concluded that there is no concept of law to be analyzed and that the expression "A legal system exists in *S*" has no clear meaning—unless such a meaning is *assigned* to it. The controversies over the nature of law, it is maintained, are just so many stipulations of definitions, proposals for the use of a phrase. Such proposals can at most be said to be convenient or inconvenient, not correct or incorrect.[2] This position we may call *conventionalism*.

We cannot settle these matters at present. It will be useful for us temporarily to proceed as if *essentialism* (the view that legal systems have an essence) is correct, and we shall attempt to supply the necessary and

---

[2] See Glanville Williams, "The Controversy Concerning the Word 'Law'," in P. Laslett, ed., *Philosophy, Politics and Society* (Oxford: Basil Blackwell, first series, 1956), 134–56. For a critique of Williams, see E. Gellner, "Contemporary Thought and Politics," *Philosophy*, 32 (1957), 353 ff. See also Herbert Morris, "Verbal Disputes and the Legal Philosophy of John Austin," *U.C.L.A. Law Rev.*, 7 (1960), 27–56.

sufficient conditions for assertions of the form "A legal system exists in *S*." The disagreement between the essentialist and conventionalist approaches will recur at a number of points in this chapter. I shall later indicate the limited kinds of context in which it would be appropriate to stipulate a meaning for "A legal system exists in *S*" (and other related expressions). Suffice it to say at present that even if essentialism is wrong, it does not follow that conventionalism is right.

THE ELEMENTS OF   I now turn to the elucidation of what it means
LEGAL SYSTEMS   to say that a legal system exists in a society. In
                           order to get clues on this, let us suppose that we are
members of a party of anthropologists studying the communal life of a
tribe of South Sea Islanders. We plan ultimately to write a book about
this society, describing therein its economy, its religious beliefs and
practices, the structure and functions of the family, and so on. Included
also will be a chapter on the law of this community, if there is any. Now
in order to carry out a systematic investigation, we must have at least a
rough idea of the data that would be relevant to it. That is, we must know,
broadly, what to look for, although we cannot be sure that we will find it.

Our first step, then, is to formulate in this light specific subjects for
inquiry. A number immediately suggest themselves. For example, mindful
of the view of many historians that dispute settlement is one of the
earliest forms of law, we would be interested in how disputes are settled
in our island community. Is there an agency, a social mechanism or
institution, for settling disputes between individuals? And if so, what
kinds of dispute will it undertake to settle, or is it unrestricted in this
respect? How are disputes brought to the attention of this agency for
purposes of settlement? Is there an adjudicative procedure like that
which prevails in our own courts, or do the procedures parallel the more
informal methods of dispute settlement that one finds among a closely
knit group of friends? Are the decisions of this agency regarded as being
merely advisory, or is there some machinery for enforcing its decisions
when a party to the dispute is recalcitrant? And so on. Clearly, on the
basis of the knowledge we may already have about our Islanders—their
"level" of social development—certain lines of inquiry will be immediately
recognized as fruitful, while others will be eliminated.

The various questions that have been posed so far—the hypothetical
lines of inquiry that call for investigation—are centered around the
existence of a particular *agency* that engages in a particular activity,
namely, the *settling of disputes*. We shall call such an agency a *jural
agency* and such an activity a *jural activity*. The chapter on law in our
book on the Islanders will contain a description of this agency, if the

society has one, and the way this jural activity is conducted. Naturally, this chapter will be concerned with much more, for there are other lines of inquiry which we would want to undertake. Some of these, it will be seen, also concern particular kinds of jural agency and jural activity.

We have noted the question of whether or not there is a mechanism for enforcing the decisions of the dispute settler. This may be generalized: How are the laws of the community enforced? The *enforcement of the laws* is another jural activity of interest to us. Is there an agency that has this task, or does the society rely upon diffuse social pressure to secure compliance? What methods are available to this end (e.g., capital punishment, ostracism, imprisonment, fines, expressions of disapproval, etc.)? In what circumstances is a wronged party allowed to resort to self-help? If there exists an agency for enforcing the laws, how is it constituted and how is its membership recruited? Is there anything like a police force, permanently on guard to prevent violations of the laws? And so on. Here also, we may be able to eliminate various items as being too unfruitful for investigation.

When we think of an agency, or perhaps some other device, for enforcing the laws, we would also ordinarily expect it to operate in conjunction with a technique for determining when infractions of the laws have taken place. This gives rise to another set of questions about the jural activity of *determining infractions of the laws* and its appropriate agency. If such an agency exists, how is it constituted? Are all heads of clans or households assigned the task of determining such infractions? What procedures, if any, govern this jural activity? Is trial by ordeal employed? Does the burden of presenting the case fall upon the accuser or the accused? And so on. Naturally, we would again avail ourselves of any information already acquired about the society before carrying out any of these lines of investigation.

At this point our attention may be drawn to another, and very important, jural activity. We have spoken of the determining of infractions and the enforcement of the laws. But what about the laws themselves? How did the laws get to be the laws of the Islanders? To put it in other terms, how were the laws made? This raises an extremely delicate topic in the study of so-called "primitive" peoples. A good many of their laws do not seem to have been made by anyone, but are simply "just there" to be handed down from one generation to the next. On the other hand, there are often legends concerning gods or wise men of the ancient past who were lawgivers to the people. In any case, as investigators, we would certainly wish to know whether there is any method whereby the laws can at least be changed. The jural activity of *making and changing the laws* certainly does occur in many societies. And we may, therefore, frame the question of whether there exists in the community some agency that engages in this activity. Naturally, if the island community has a chieftain or a council of elders, we would want to know whether either is active in this regard. Here too, a set of questions would be generated about such an agency and the conducting of this jural activity. Are there any procedures that govern this activity? Does the council, if there is one, operate under majority rule, etc.? What factors motivate the introduction of changes or the making of new laws? How are such laws made known to the members of the society? And so on. We would again fall back upon any knowledge we have concerning the community before undertaking to answer these questions. Although this area of research may prove relatively barren for our chapter on law, it has important philosophical ramifications, as will be seen.

Finally, the chapter must contain at least a summary account of *the laws* themselves. What are the laws? What kinds of behavior do they govern? Are the laws codified in a particular written or oral format? Is a special terminology used in formulating the laws? These are only some of the important questions that we may choose to deal with.

Our Islander example provides us with clues for the elucidation of what it means to say that a legal system exists in a society (alternatively, with clues for what is implied in assertions of the form "A legal system exists in society *S*"). And this in turn will enable us to formulate the issues that are inherent in the problem of the nature of law.

In line with the above discussion, the following proposal naturally suggests itself. An assertion of the form

A legal system exists in *S*

is true if, and only if, the following conditions are satisfied:

1. There are laws in *S*.
2. There exists in *S* an agency for changing and making the laws.
3. There exists in *S* an agency for determining infractions of the laws.
4. There exists in *S* an agency for enforcing the laws.
5. There exists in S an agency for settling disputes between individuals.

Each of these items is a necessary condition for the truth of the original assertion, and jointly they are sufficient for its truth.

Before we discuss the adequacy of this proposal, there are several important points that merit our attention.

The correspondence of the proposed elucidation to the process of inquiry adopted in the Islander example is clear. The study of the law of this community was framed in terms of a set of questions concerning four kinds of jural agencies, four coordinate kinds of jural activities, and the laws of the society. These questions are clues to the meaning of assertions of the form "A legal system exists in *S*." Now though it might have been possible to reach the above proposal by first fixing in our mind the notion of the existence of a legal system in a society and then cogitating upon this notion, it is apparent that such a procedure is haphazard at best, and holds out little chance of success. The analytical strategy that we, however, have adopted (namely, of assuming the perspective of an orderly inquiry into the legal system of a society) is clearly more advantageous. For—and this is the essential point—in attempting to understand a notion it is helpful to see what questions we would ask about anything to which we are considering applying that notion. The proposed elucidation, it should be noticed, is based upon the five *groups* of questions that were raised about the island community. In each group there are a number of rather specific questions concerning the organization of the agencies, their modes of operation, the conducting of the jural activities, and the laws. Although some of these specific questions are of philosophical interest, they seem to have no bearing on whether a legal system exists in the society, but relate instead to the distinctive characteristics of the given system. The five items of the proposed elucidation derive from the attempt to isolate from such extraneous matters just those elements that are constituents of the notion of the existence of a legal system. Obviously, societies S' and S'' may each have a legal system, and yet these systems may differ in many respects. We shall shortly consider whether differences regarding the very presence or absence of any of the five items may obtain among legal systems. This issue bears upon the adequacy of our proposed elucidation.

THE CONCEPT OF A LEGAL SYSTEM   The preceding remarks help to establish the initial plausibility of the proposed elucidation of "A legal system exists in S." There is an interrelationship between the anthropological study of the law of a community and our (perhaps somewhat inchoate) intuitive notion of the existence of a legal system in a society. Just as our concept of the existence of a legal system is clarified by reference to the questions we would ask about a purported instance of the concept, so also such questions are affected by our pre-analytic notion of the existence of a legal system. But there is another factor which has an influence on both of these and which also helps in establishing the plausibility of our proposal: the legal system of our own community. This provides us with a *clear case* of the existence of a legal system. The most general features of this case certainly appear to be the five elements of the above analysis. One is, of course, entitled to advance other candidates for the general features, and to maintain, for example, that there are more than four jural agencies and activities. Any specific candidate merits consideration, and this may lead to the proposing of a more elaborate elucidation. It would be unsafe to be dogmatic about such matters, and I am only arguing the plausibility of our proposal. Naturally, to affirm its plausibility is hardly to claim that it is faultless. It is necessary to add, however, that the problems which the proposal enables us to expose would, as we shall see, remain as legitimate problems whether or not the elucidation is found to be adequate.

Although initially plausible, the analysis of some concept or the elucidation of the meaning of some expression may be inadequate in two ways. It may be *too weak* or *too strong*. According to the traditional analysis

X is human

if, and only if,

  i] X is rational.
  ii] X is an animal.

But if, for example, condition (i) were removed, clearly the resulting analysis would be too weak. The remaining condition is satisfied by chickens, who are nonhuman, as well as by men. (Obviously, if the analysis completely failed to subsume the class of humans it would have no color of initial plausibility.) On the other hand, if

  iii] X is Greek-speaking

were added to the above set, clearly the resulting analysis would be too strong. Furthermore, even if it were *coincidentally* the case that all men spoke Greek, the resulting analysis would still be too strong. For we would wish to maintain that if by hypothesis someone were to satisfy conditions (i) and (ii), he would qualify as a human being even though he did not speak Greek. One can *conceive* of non-Greek-speaking humans, but not nonrational humans, according to the ancient view. Considerations analogous to these apply to the proposed elucidation of "A legal system exists in S."

Of course, it is easier to show that an analysis (or elucidation) is either too weak or too strong than to prove that an analysis is adequate. Proof is generally out of the question. The best we can do is to pay careful attention to our common language and common thinking on the particular subject. By sifting through a variety of examples, we may be able to fend off allegations as to weakness or stringency.

We are not yet in a position to determine whether there is a respect in which our proposed elucidation is too weak. This hardly appears to be the case, for it seems true to say of any society in which the five conditions obtain (e.g., a clear case) that a legal system exists therein. But a rather complicated issue is concealed here, so we shall have to postpone the discussion of this point.[3]

On the other hand, we can usefully take up the question of whether or not the proposed elucidation of "A legal system exists in S" is too strong. I shall argue that this is in fact the case and, further, that essentialism, in the form in which it was originally explained, cannot be maintained.

Consider the Islander example. Suppose investigation reveals that in the island society there are laws, an agency for determining infractions of the laws, an agency for enforcing the laws, and an agency for settling disputes between individuals—but there is no agency for changing or making the laws. This would hardly be surprising in a relatively simple and static society. (This is not to say that the laws do not change; rather, the process of change is not deliberate.) Would we deny that there is a legal system in the island society? I hardly think so. We would instead maintain that there *is* a legal system there, although it lacks one of the features that are characteristic of the clear cases. Not every case falling under a concept or expression need have all the features—or even all the central features—of the clear cases. The presence in S' of an agency for changing and making the laws obviously counts in favor of the assertion that a legal system exists in S', but its absence need not deter us from making this assertion so long as other conditions are fulfilled. This point deserves to be underscored because many legal philosophers who differ widely on many important issues nevertheless focus their theories of law upon such an agency. Theories of this sort will be discussed in the next chapter.

It is clear from the above that the second element of the proposed elucidation of "A legal system exists in S" can be dispensed with when the other conditions are fulfilled, and therefore that our proposal is too strong. But it does not follow that this element is eliminable in every circumstance.

What we must do now is consider a supposition analogous to the preceding example for each of the other three jural agencies in turn. Using the numerals attached to each of the elements of the analysis (see p. 11), the cases we are supposing are:

a. 1, 3, 4, 5 (the case just considered)
b. 1, 2, 4, 5
c. 1, 2, 3, 5
d. 1, 2, 3, 4

For each of these we must again ask: Would we assert that there is a legal system in the island society? (How well such systems function is not at issue here.) Perhaps there will not be complete agreement on the answers.

[3] See the discussion of "minimum content," pp. 21–22.

For my own part, I have little hesitation in answering this question in the affirmative, and I think it must be admitted that the attribution of a legal system to the society is, at the very least, highly plausible in each of these cases.

JURAL COMPLEXITY   We shall shortly turn to the significance of this view for the disagreement between the essentialist and conventionalist approaches. A few comments on the above cases are in order first.

Case b. The agency for determining infractions of the laws, whose absence is being supposed, usually operates in conjunction with an agency for enforcing the laws. What I have in mind, therefore, is that there might not be a separate agency for determining infractions whose activity is distinct from the activity of enforcing the laws. It is like a case of police and policing without the criminal courts. This, of course, raises the question of how the activity in question—which is different from the mere on-the-spot imposition of "summary justice" and crime prevention— is to be characterized. This is a problem of the theory of law which we cannot take up at present. Now, the presence of this agency would clearly support the claim that S has a legal system, but so long as the other conditions are fulfilled its absence does not refute the claim.

Case c. This is the most controversial of the cases. Two points are involved and they are interconnected. First, in the absence of an agency for enforcing the laws, how shall the laws of the society be identified? It might seem that there is no way of distinguishing the laws of the society from other norms except in relation to an agency of enforcement. But given the presence of the other agencies, no difficulty presents itself on this score. Second, the absence of an agency of enforcement might seem to rob the laws of their *jural* character, reducing them to the status of other social norms. This point, I admit, has some force. Nevertheless, when the other agencies exist, I would maintain that the society has a sufficient degree of *jural complexity* that allows us to assert that a legal system exists in the society.

Case d. The absence of an agency for settling disputes between individuals raises no problem for us. We would of course be surprised to find such an agency lacking among the Islanders, and we would search for other mechanisms for dispute settlement. (In a later chapter, we shall examine various kinds of dispute settling.)

From this survey we may conclude (1) that the existence of any one of the four jural agencies may be advanced in *support* of the claim that a legal system exists in a given society, and (2) that the existence of any particular agency is not a necessary condition for the truth of such a claim. Our proposed elucidation of "A legal system exists in S" is clearly too strong. Instead of a single set of necessary conditions that are jointly sufficient for the truth of assertions of this form, we have four sets of sufficient conditions (a) to (d).

But I think we can go even further than this. Instead of taking merely one of the jural agencies to be absent from the island community we can suppose that two of the four agencies are lacking. There are six cases of this sort, but we shall not examine them in detail here. It seems to me that it would be plausible in each of these cases to assert that a legal system exists in the given society. Thus, even fewer conditions would have to be satisfied in order to establish the assertion. We only need the existence of laws and any two of the jural agencies. I do not think, however, that we can weaken the set of conditions to the point of allowing that a legal system exists in a society when there are laws and only one of the agencies.

The moral to be drawn from this survey is that law or (more precisely) the existence of a legal system is *not* an invariant type of phenomenon. To the extent that this negative claim is basic to the conventionalist's criticism of the essentialist approach, I would agree with the conventionalist. *But* it does not follow that the conventionalist position is entirely correct if it means that one is free to stipulate any meaning one wishes for the word "law" or any set of conditions for the truth of statements of the form "A legal system exists in S." For our claim amounts to saying that legal systems may differ from one another in the rich variety of respects that have been spelled out in our survey. Thus, there may be two systems L' and L'' in societies S' and S'' that do not have the same kinds of jural agency. Yet L' and L'' may both be legal systems. Nevertheless, all legal systems, as far as our present account is concerned, do share in certain very general features—namely, laws and jural complexity.[4] The reader will certainly have noticed that the existence of laws was posited in all of these cases. Laws are a necessary element of every legal system. A "lawless" legal system is inconceivable—it would be like *Hamlet* without the Prince. The valid point against the essentialist is that there is more than one way in which jural complexity can be attained. The concept of a legal system may be instantiated in a number of different ways. Still, the presence in a society of any of the agencies *is* relevant to the assertion that the society has a legal system. The position adopted here is one of modified essentialism.

I close this discussion with a caution. Nothing that I have said must

---

[4] Thus, if an Islander-English dictionary translated the Islander term "begal fystem" by the English "legal system," we could not on this basis alone infer what the constituents of the Island system are other than its having laws and jural complexity.

be taken as implying that there are no contexts in which it is legitimate to stipulate a meaning for "A legal system exists in *S*" or for other related terms. We shall have occasion to advert to this point in the next section.

We now, finally, turn to the elements of the *problem of the nature of law*. Some of them have already been touched upon. And it should also be clear that we have been doing a fair amount of legal philosophy during the course of examining the adequacy of our proposed elucidation of "A legal system exists in *S*." This examination has, among other things, also provided us with models for comparing different theories of the nature of law. Our main purpose, however, was to elicit the problems in a systematic manner, and the proposal helps us do just this. As it now stands, the proposal still includes the five conditions:

1. There are laws in *S*.
2. There exists in *S* an agency for making and changing the laws.
3. There exists in *S* an agency for determining infractions of the laws.
4. There exists in *S* an agency for enforcing the laws.
5. There exists in *S* an agency for settling disputes between individuals.

The first of these conditions would have to be satisfied by any society for it to have a legal system. The satisfaction of conditions (2) to (5) is relevant to establishing such an assertion. There is also the further proviso that the society must have a sufficient degree of jural complexity.

We may now ask for each of these five conditions: Under what circumstances shall it be held to be satisfied?

For the sake of economy, we cannot mount separate attacks on each of the five conditions. Nor is it necessary to do so. The basic issues—the basic components of the problem of the nature of law—revolve around (1) the analysis of the concept of *a law* (or laws), (2) the analysis of the concept of *jural agency,* and (3) the characterization of the general features of the various *jural activities*. No hard and fast boundaries separate these topics, and we shall have to cross the lines in discussing the first one. Most of our attention, therefore, will be given to it.[5]

LAWS   There are three main problems about laws: that of their identification and existence, legal obligation, and the content of a legal system.

We have already touched upon the first of these. It will be recalled that in our anthropological example one of our tasks was the giving of

---

[5] Because of limitations of space, topic 3 will not be discussed separately, but rather incidentally to the treatment of the other topics. Chapter Six takes up one of the jural activities in some detail.

a summary account of the laws of the Islanders. This may turn out to be a formidable affair, but not because the laws of this society are so complicated that they do not lend themselves to summary exposition. The difficulty may be, rather, to distinguish the laws of the society from other "law-like" objects: conventions, social rules, precepts, taboos, models of conduct, customs, mores, fashions, usages, practices, routines, and habits. How can we, for example, distinguish the laws from what is, loosely speaking, done "as a rule" in the society?

It is useful to consider one of the more extreme cases, the Nuer, a Nilotic people residing in the Sudan. The Nuer, if they have any government at all, appear to have as little of it as any society anywhere, according to Professor Lucy Mair. There is nothing corresponding to courts and policemen. But although it takes little to make Nuers fight, they are not constantly engaged in a Hobbesian war of all against all. Mair cites the anthropologist Evans-Pritchard as describing the Nuer as living in a condition of "ordered anarchy." Certain forms of conduct are regarded as "offenses"; there is a sense of "mine" and "thine"; and when an individual is "wronged," either in his person or property, the group is expected to aid him in securing compensation from the offender. Often this consists in the recognition of the "right" of the wronged individual to fight—to use force—in order to secure compensation. There are also customs that set limits to self-help and the feud. But there is no sense of the group's being "authorized" to act in someone's behalf, and there is no individual who is recognized as having authority to say whether fighting is permissible or to command that it should cease.[6]

Now, this is an extreme case, not only because it raises in a stark fashion the question of how the laws of the society are to be picked out from this set of practices or conventions but also because it is problematic as to how these practices are to be characterized in the first place. Are they social rules? Social habits? Or should they all be characterized as laws? I raise this example because it is important to see that as *anthropologists* we have ways of avoiding these difficulties. Suppose that upon investigation our Islanders are found to have a culture similar to that of the Nuer. We may simply decide, in writing our book on the Islanders, to *retitle* what was to be a chapter on the law of the Islanders. The word "law" need never appear in it. Instead of speaking of the enforcement of the laws, we will speak of the handling of deviance, for example.

There is also another alternative open to us, as anthropologists. We are free to adopt what we would regard as appropriate definitions of the key terms. Thus, "*x* is a law in *S*" might be stipulated as meaning "*x* is a general practice in *S*, and deviations from *x* are subject to severe censure

---

[6] See Lucy Mair, *Primitive Government* (Baltimore: Penguin Books, 1964), Chapter 1.

by the members of *S*." The fact that this could result in collapsing together what are called laws, morality, social rules, customs, etc. occasions no trouble. The readers of our book will be clear on what we mean by "the laws" of the society. We might also go farther than this and stipulate a meaning for "A legal system exists in *S*" for the purposes of writing our book on the Islanders.

But this freedom to introduce any definitions that we find convenient holds only for *short-term* purposes. The defined term, in the example just given, would function for us as an abbreviation of the longer and more cumbersome expression—but only within the scope of our book on the Islanders. It is only within such restrictions as to context that the conventionalist approach is legitimate.[7]

As philosophers we seek *long-term* definitions and elucidations of the meanings of words—which is why we often speak of analyzing concepts —and we cannot employ the devices open to us as writers of a book on anthropology.[8] Philosophical definitions, in any event, are the results rather than the starting points of inquiry, though they are not always expounded in this manner. There is no guarantee that such results—in terms of a set of necessary and sufficient conditions—are always attainable. This seems especially true in the case of the term "laws." Of course, a philosopher may *propose* a definition for long-term use. This is quite different from freely legislating or stipulating a definition that is to hold within a restricted scope over which the definer has control. Of a proposal we may ask whether it is good or bad. We may accept or reject such a proposal. In either case, *reasons* will have to be given. Sometimes, for example, a definition may be "refuted" by producing a clear counter-example to it.

Long-term definitions of the term "laws" (or conditions for the truth of expressions of the form "*x* is a law," or analyses of the concept of law) are intended to capture the widest group of applications of the term while preserving distinctions that are intuitively recognized. There is a sense, therefore, in which we must admit that "the real difficulty is not one of definition at all but of isolating the thing to be defined. It is from this point that the crowd of existing definitions diverge."[9]

The philosopher's problem is set by the fact that laws generally

---

7 Anthropologists do not always choose to employ this device. For a discussion of the problem, see Bronislaw Malinowski's introduction to H. Ian Hogbin, *Law and Order in Polynesia* (New York: Harcourt, Brace and Co., 1934); Paul Bohannan, "The Differing Realms of Law," in P. Bohannan, ed., *Law and Warfare: Studies in the Anthropology of Conflict* (Garden City: Natural History Press, 1964), pp. 43–56. See also A. A. Schiller, "Law," in R. A. Lystad, ed., *The African World: A Survey of Social Research* (New York: Praeger, 1967), pp. 167 ff.

8 See Gellner, "Contemporary Thought and Politics."

9 Albert Kocourek, *An Introduction to the Science of Law* (Boston: Little, Brown and Co., 1930), p. 216.

(although perhaps not always) have a number of characteristics that are shared by nonlaws. For example, laws, like moral rules and the rules of games, require or forbid the performance of given kinds of conduct. This raises the question: In what sense do laws make it obligatory to perform or omit some act? Like the rules of morality and customary social rules, laws are used as guides to conduct; and like customary rules, but unlike moral rules, laws have force or validity within a restricted territorial scope. How then shall laws be distinguished from moral rules on the one hand and customary norms on the other? Both laws and customs are subject to enforcement in some sense, but is there anything special about the enforcement of laws?

One of the legal philosopher's tasks, then, is to supply a formula (or definition, or analysis) for selecting the laws of a society from among the objects having properties in common with laws and with which laws might be confused.[10] Such a formula is often spoken of as a *theory* of law. In the following chapter we shall examine some representative theories from two main traditions in legal philosophy. As we shall see, some of the theories assign special significance to certain of the jural agencies.

THE VALIDITY OF LAWS   One of the main ways of dealing with the question of the existence of laws in a society is in terms of the idea of the validity of laws. The laws that exist in a society are presumably those that are valid in it. Thus, given a set of "law-like" sentences (e.g., a set of rules), we can ask whether this set represents the valid laws of a given society. Four types of criterion seem relevant to this, one or the other of which has been emphasized in major theories of law. We shall note them briefly here.

Behavioral Criteria. It would indeed be difficult to maintain that some set of rules comprises the valid laws of a given society if the actual behavior of the members were completely indifferent to them. As an analogy, suppose a group of card players as a society in miniature. A question arises as to what game they are playing, i.e., what are the rules of this society. If their game behavior were not largely in conformity with the rules of bridge, we would hardly say that they are playing bridge. That is to say, in order to assert the validity (and existence) of the rules in the game-society, the set of rules must be effective in the minimal sense

---

[10] One of the devices sometimes used for supplying this formula is a canonical form for expressing a law. Such a form, it is maintained, allows one to state the "real content" of a law in a way that shows forth its jural nature. A classic example is provided by Hans Kelsen, whose theory will be discussed in the next chapter.

that the behavior conforms to the rules. So also for the laws of a society; the laws must be effective in order to assert their validity, except that we do not expect the laws to be completely effective.

Psychological-Behavioral Criteria. Some writers maintain that such behavioral considerations at best constitute a necessary condition for the validity (and existence) of laws in a society. These theorists require that the members should have critical *attitudes* toward their conduct with respect to the laws. The valid laws, in other words, are laws that are *normative* for the conduct of the members, i.e., used as guides to action.

Deontic Criteria. Some writers believe that such psychological-behavioral considerations are also insufficient. The valid laws of a society, they maintain, are not merely those that are used as guides. Furthermore this is not always necessary. What is crucial is for the laws to be *binding* on its members. A purported law that the members have no obligation to obey is not, on this view, a valid law.

The last of these three types of criteria raises some of the most heated controversy in the philosophy of law. How is this obligation to be understood? Four leading interpretations have been propounded. They turn up singly or in various combinations in theories we shall consider later. On the first interpretation, laws are binding upon a society when they are *enforced.* In a sense, "might is right." This position presupposes the existence of an agency for enforcing the laws. On the second interpretation—an extension of the psychological-behavioral approach—laws are binding when they are *recognized as binding* by the members. The members of our miniature bridge society guide their conduct by the rules of bridge because they *accept* the rules as binding upon them. So also in the case of laws. This is a version of the social contract theory of the state. Following our game analogy we may call this theory of the obligation of laws the "contract theory of social bridge." On the third interpretation, the bindingness of laws is a unique kind of obligation which attaches to laws that are made in accordance with the the *formal* requirements for making laws in the given society. This position presupposes the existence of an agency for making the laws and something like a constitution. On the fourth interpretation, laws are binding upon the members of a society when the members have a *moral obligation* to conform to the laws. Such an obligation holds when the laws satisfy certain ethical standards—for example, a principle of justice.

Minimum Content. This factor deserves separate mention, although it is often associated with the fourth interpretation, above. The notion of the existence of laws in a society, it might be argued, is not adequately represented by any of the factors, taken singly or in combination, hitherto expounded. This notion is not so unspecific. For (according to this view) when we think of laws existing in a society, we think of them as including laws of a very basic sort. For example, there must be laws that prohibit the free use of violence in the society. Such laws constitute the *minimum content* of every set of laws. On the other hand, it might plausibly be urged that the requirement of specific minimum content—if it is adopted at all—is not a condition for the existence of laws in a society, but a separate condition for the existence of a legal system. If this is correct, the elucidation of "A legal system exists in *S*" originally proposed is, in this regard, too weak. In any case, it should be noted that the idea of minimum content is subject to alternative interpretations, which we shall consider in our discussion of theories of the nature of law.

JURAL AGENCIES AND JURAL ACTIVITIES   Our task in this section is to delineate issues that arise in the analysis of what it means to speak, in general, of the presence of a jural agency and of jural activity in a society. The two are so intimately related that they cannot be taken up separately. Many of the points mentioned in the discussion of the criteria for the existence and validity of laws turn up again in the discussion of these issues.

The fundamental problem, basic to the analysis of both jural agencies and jural activities, may be readily stated, using an example taken from Hans Kelsen. Suppose that we come upon two separate cases of one man killing another. Suppose further that in all behavioral and psychological respects the two acts are perfectly alike: each actor, with venom in his heart, kills his enemy with a sword. Now, it does not follow that there can be no difference between the two cases; in fact, one is a pure case of murder, while the other is not. This is possible because one of the killers (the latter) is the state executioner who is carrying out the sentence of a court. His act is the act of an *official*—he is a jural agent—acting in an official capacity, and it is an instance of a jural activity.

The reader can easily construct other parallel cases of this sort. We are aware of a difference between the case of a policeman waving us through a red light and the case of a private citizen so doing. If we obey the former, we will be doing something legal, while if we obey the latter, we will be behaving illegally. Similarly, one acknowledges a difference between my saying that *Y* is guilty of a violation of a law and a judge's pronouncing *Y* guilty of such a violation. My saying so has no jural significance; it is without legal effect. And as a final but very important example, we all acknowledge that there is a difference between my saying (or even a law professor's saying) that parking next to fire hydrants is prohibited and the case of the legislator saying this. Both the law professor and I might be *correct* in what we say, but the legislator's saying so *makes* it the law. The crux of the difference in each of these pairs is the notion of the performance of a jural activity by a jural agent.

The concepts of jural activity and jural agency are in some respects correlative. In order to identify some act as an instance of a jural activity, it must be an act of an appropriate sort. It must be the kind of act that would be engaged in by someone who is enforcing a law, determining an infraction of a law, making or changing a law, or settling a dispute. (It is no easy task to specify the kinds of conduct that typically fall under these headings.) Secondly, a jural agent is someone who engages in the appropriate activities. But what makes him a jural agent, and his acts jural activities, in his *authoritative* status in the society.

It is in the analysis of this status that the approaches mentioned in connection with the validity of laws in a society reduplicate themselves, although the formulations are more complex. We shall not go through the entire list. The behavioral position can serve as a representative example. On this view it would be true to say that X is a jural agent in S if X's appropriate acts are and will be effective in the society. Of course, it would be foolish to demand that every single one of his acts be effective; this would set too high a standard for the existence of jural agencies. Nor could we determine the authoritative standing of a single act on the basis of its own effectiveness. Rather, the standing of an act as a jural act is determined with reference to its place in a *pattern* of effective acts of the appropriate sort.

Specific mention should also be made here of the analogue to the *formal* deontic position, which has been highly influential in this century because it was developed in conscious opposition to the other approaches. According to this position the existence of laws in a society presupposes the existence of a jural agency for making the laws. The creation of laws, further, is regulated by laws that establish when the jural agent is acting in an official capacity so that his pronouncements should constitute jural acts of law-making. Such laws are called *laws of competence* or *power-delegating laws*, and their existence is, in effect, a condition for the existence of the particular jural agency. This approach has the apparently paradoxical consequence that the existence of laws is a precondition for the existence of laws. (In less technical terms, this position maintains that the legislature derives its authority from the constitution. The question then arises: Whence does the constitution derive its validity?)

Each of the positions has its underlying rationale and its special difficulties. We shall discuss these matters within the context of specific theories of law in the following chapter.

CHAPTER TWO

The Nature of Law: Theories

It is now time to turn to some of the major attempts to deal with issues identified in Chapter One. What are laws? What are the criteria for their existence and validity? Must laws satisfy certain moral requirements in order to be binding? What connection, if any, is there between the existence of laws and the various jural agencies and activities? What are the conditions for the existence of jural agencies? Instead of taking up these questions one by one, we shall focus upon two traditions in legal philosophy—legal positivism and natural law—and see how they are treated by important representatives of each tradition. These traditions are not monolithic: in determining the existence of laws and jural agencies, the previously mentioned criteria (behavioral, deontic, etc.) are differently emphasized by theorists who belong to the same tradition.

LEGAL POSITIVISM: AUSTIN   By way of getting our bearings, it is useful to begin by contrasting the traditions in a vivid manner. An early intimation of legal positivism is to be found in a fragment of a classical statement preserved in Justinian's

Digest: "What pleases the Prince has the force of law." Putting it in more modern terms, whatever is enacted by the lawmaking agency is the law in the society. This thesis would be generally accepted by contemporary legal positivists. And they would also agree with the nineteenth-century English writer John Austin that "the existence of law is one thing; its merit or demerit is another." [1] With varying degrees of emphasis, natural law theorists reject both of these theses. They tend to maintain that law-making is a purposive activity that must satisfy certain moral require-ments in order for it to have laws as its outcome. Secondly, they tend to maintain that the question of the existence of laws cannot be com-pletely separated from the question of their moral obligatoriness or moral quality. Thus, natural law theorists adopt, or come close to adopt-ing, a moral-deontic position.

It is essential that we should immediately note that Austin's quoted statement does not imply that laws cannot be morally evaluated; quite the contrary. Austin was a utilitarian. Like Jeremy Bentham, Austin thought it possible to construct a "science of legislation" based upon the Principle of Utility (the greatest happiness principle), which would pro-vide guidance to the legislator. But, following Bentham, he held that we should clearly distinguish those laws (good or bad) that actually *do* exist in a society from laws that might exist if the legislator were properly en-lightened. Secondly, he held that the laws should also be distinguished from the society's prevailing rules of morality ("positive morality"). (Recall our South Sea Island example.) Austin wished to give an account of the general features of legal systems, and therefore set out to determine "the province of jurisprudence."

The "key word" in jurisprudence, according to Austin, is *command*. The laws of a society are the general commands of the sovereign—the supreme political authority—to govern the conduct of the society's mem-bers. The sovereign is that individual, or determinate group of individuals (a) toward whom the bulk of the society has a *habit of obedience,* and (b) who is in turn not habitually obedient to any one else. A command of the sovereign (a law) imposes an *obligation* or *duty* on the persons who are directed to act or not to act in a certain way. In terms of the criteria discussed in the previous chapter, we may say that Austin's theory com-bines elements of the behavioral or psychological-behavioral (according to how we understand the term "habit") and deontic approaches to the existence of laws and the lawmaking agency. Austin's interpretation of the deontic element is brought out in his analysis of "commands."

What is a command? Austin's definition has two components. A com-

---

[1] *The Province of Jurisprudence Determined*, first published 1832 (New York: Noonday Press, 1954), p. 184. Selections from writers discussed in this chapter may be found in M. P. Golding, ed., *The Nature of Law* (New York: Random House, 1966).

mand is first of all a signification of desire that someone should act or refrain from acting in a certain way. It will usually (though not necessarily) be formulated in the imperative mood. Obviously, however, not every expression of desire is a command. If I say "Am I ever thirsty!" I thereby signify my desire for drink but I haven't issued a command. A command, therefore, is distinguished by Austin from other significations of desire "by this peculiarity: that the party to whom it is directed is liable to evil from the other, in case he comply not with the desire." [2] Commands are orders backed by threats. It is in virtue of threatened evils, sanctions, that expressions of desire not only constitute commands but also impose an obligation or duty to act in the prescribed ways. "Command" and "duty," says Austin, are correlative terms. The command situation, then, involves the relationships of superiority and inferiority. That laws emanate from superiors is considered by Austin to be a necessary truth.

Austin's theory, with its great stress on the agency for making the laws, was quick to find its critics. We can consider only a few objections.[3] One of the most damaging criticisms, I think, is brought out by Sir Henry Sumner Maine. We need not accept all of Maine's account of the evolution of legal institutions in order to agree with him that explicit *legislation* comes at its later stages. Legislation presupposes not only a centralization of authority that is lacking in many communities but also a "new order" of ideas. In the classic oriental despotism, the chieftain could command anything, and the smallest disobedience might be followed by death. He raised armies, collected taxes, and executed his enemies. But, says Maine, the chieftain never made a law. Although he issued particular commands, he would not have dreamed of changing the rules, the immemorial usages, under which his subjects lived. Laws, therefore, are not necessarily to be identified with *made* laws.[4]

There are two ways in which Austin can reply to this objection. The first is to say that the regime of rules referred to by Maine is not a legal system but, at best, a positive morality. If the rules are such as to impose obligations, they presuppose a commander, Austin would argue. But this reply, which involves Austin's command theory of obligation (including moral obligation), is implausible, as we shall see. In order to hold that laws derive their obligatoriness from sanctions, one needs only to pre-

---

2 Ibid., p. 14.

3 An important issue that we cannot consider is Austin's denial, as a consequence of his theory, of jural status to international law.

4 *Early History of Institutions*, 7th ed. (London: John Murray, 1897), pp. 375–86. For an elaboration of this criticism in relation to modern systems, see Lon L. Fuller, *Anatomy of the Law* (New York: American Library, 1969).

suppose the existence of jural agencies for their enforcement. It is not necessary to assume that the laws are also someone's commands.

A second course is suggested by Austin's followers. Let us grant, they say, that Austin's theory is incorrect as applied to primitive legal systems; it is, nevertheless, accurate for modern ones. Thus in so-called systems of municipal law, customary rules of conduct, no matter how immemorial, are not to be accorded the status of law unless they receive the imprimatur of the sovereign. This reply, however, aside from conceding a very major point, does not relieve Austin of all his difficulties.

Austin insisted that when the sovereign is a body of individuals, it must be a determinate body. That is to say, there is a rule (e.g., an election law) whereby it may be determined for any individual in the society whether or not he is a member of the sovereign body. The reason for this insistence is that only a determinate body can be said to express its will, signify its desire. Who, then, is the sovereign in a federal system? Austin's answer for the United States is "two-thirds of the Congress and three-fourths of the States," for it is this "body" that has the ultimate authority to change the Constitution. But it seems absurd to say that this (shifting) body wills, or desires, the laws. Second, in the modern legislature, the laws that are enacted are meant to bind not only the ordinary citizen but also the legislators themselves. On Austin's theory we would have to conceive of the legislators as commanding, ordering, and threatening themselves. But this also seems absurd. Even if we confine Austin's theory to a hypothetical King Rex, an absolute monarch who is above the law, there is difficulty. When Rex I dies and his son Rex II assumes the throne in virtue of a law of succession, we cannot conceive of that law as a command of the king. Furthermore, it may take some time before we can say that the members of the society have built up a habit of obedience, or are generally obedient, toward Rex II. During the interim the society continues to be governed by laws; but they cannot be said to be the commands of the sovereign in Austin's sense. I think enough has been said to show that if we wish to regard laws as commands, they must be "depsychologized," as Hans Kelsen says. That is to say, we should not necessarily regard laws as the expressions of someone's desires.

COMMANDS AND OBLIGATIONS   Two further objections should be considered. The first, which is from Professor Lon L. Fuller, is part of a broad attack on legal positivism.[5] Law (or, perhaps more strictly, lawmaking) in Fuller's view is the enterprise of

[5] Lon L. Fuller, *The Morality of Law*, rev. ed. (New Haven: Yale University Press, 1969).

subjecting human conduct to the governance of rules. Abstractly stated, this is consistent with Austin. But Fuller goes on to point out that there are radical forms of "legal pathology" which may infect the attempt at regulation of conduct. Even confining ourselves again to the simple situation of King Rex, there are eight ways in which Rex can fail to make law: (1) failure to achieve rules at all, so that every issue must be decided on an *ad hoc* basis, (2) failure to publicize or make available to the affected party the rules that he is expected to observe, (3) abuse of retroactive legislation, (4) failure to make the rules understandable, (5) enactment of contradictory rules, (6) enactment of rules that require conduct beyond the power of the affected party, (7) introduction of such frequent changes in the rules that the subject cannot orient his actions by them, and (8) lack of congruence between the rules as announced and their actual administration. There are, therefore, certain conditions that must be met in order to accomplish the subjection of conduct to rules. It is incorrect simply to identify lawmaking with Rex's issuing of commands. (Later on we shall examine Fuller's interpretation of the conditions for successful lawmaking.)

The second line of criticism comes from Professor H. L. A. Hart, who argues that Austin's analysis confuses having an obligation to do something with being obliged (forced) to do it.[6] When a gunman sticks a gun in my back and says "Hand over your wallet," he has issued an order backed by a threat. I might describe this situation by saying that I was *obliged*—had no choice but—to hand over my wallet, but I would hardly say that I had an *obligation* to do so. Hart also points out that whether someone has an obligation to do something on a particular occasion is independent of the likelihood of his incurring the threatened evil on the particular occasion. The connection between sanctions or coercion and obligation, therefore, is not to be explained by the lawmaker's use of force, threatened or actual. For this still leaves us at the level of being obliged rather than having an obligation. What is required instead, according to Hart, are *rules* that confer authority or power on persons to prescribe behavior and to visit breaches of the prescriptions with the appropriate "evils."

So far our discussion has been rather negative. It seems to me that Austin has no response to these criticisms other than a modification of his theory. Its contours may be suggested. Hart's criticism does show, I think, that the correlativity between command and duty breaks down. Austin, however, might easily concede the point that the sovereign (the state or government) is simply the "gunman writ large." What distinguishes the tax collector, who in effect sticks a gun in my back when

---

[6] "Legal and Moral Obligation," in A. I. Melden, ed., *Essays in Moral Philosophy* (Seattle: University of Washington Press, 1958), pp. 82–107.

he sends me his bill, from the ordinary gunman is that the former is acting under the color of a (depsychologized) general command of the sovereign, who must be conceived as combining both the lawmaking and law-enforcing agencies. The sovereign's commands are laws because they are generally enforceable, though enforcement may fail in a particular case. It is the situation of the "gunman writ large" that characterizes a general command as a law and as imposing a *legal* obligation. In this way, the correlativity between command and duty is restored.

One may question, however, the usefulness of the term "legal obligation" in this connection. Does it point to anything more than a grandiose kind of coercive system, and if so, why retain it? An exponent of traditional natural law doctrines would argue that there is no kind of obligation that is entirely separable from moral obligation. But Austin cannot allow for any necessary linkage between legal and moral obligation because "the existence of law is one thing; its merit or demerit is another." Unfortunately, Austin's extended comment on this tenet of legal positivism serves to muddy the waters.

The context is a discussion of a passage in Blackstone's *Commentaries* according to which human laws are of no validity if they are contrary to the laws of God. Now, says Austin, if this means that positive laws ought to be framed so as to conform to divine law, he would agree. But Blackstone seems to mean that a law which conflicts with divine law is not binding or obligatory, and therefore is not a law. This is "stark nonsense," as anyone who violates a law on this ground will be shown when the threatened punishment is inflicted upon him. From this it would seem that Austin identifies the bindingness of the law with its enforceability. Austin also goes on to castigate Blackstone for having mischievously abused language. The laws of God, whose index is the Principle of Utility, are uncertain; so that what appears pernicious to one person may appear beneficial to another. Austin therefore concludes that to proclaim generally that "all laws which are pernicious or contrary to the will of God are void and not to be tolerated, is to preach anarchy. . . ." [7] With this statement Austin comes very close to revealing himself as a crypto-idealist, to use the late Felix Cohen's term. That is, he seems to invest all laws with a kind of moral imperativeness: the law is the law, it is morally binding, and there is a moral duty to obey it. If this is Austin's view, then legal obligation is more than just enforceability, and Austin has transformed his legal positivism into an *ideology*, as Professor Norberto Bobbio would put it. [8]

[7] Austin, *The Province of Jurisprudence Determined*, p. 186.

[8] Felix Cohen, *Ethical Systems and Legal Ideals* (Ithaca: Cornell University Press, 1959); Norberto Bobbio, "Sur le positivisme juridique," in *Mélanges Paul Roubier* (Paris: Dalloz et Sirey, 1961), Vol. I, 53–73.

It may be possible to save Austin by the introduction of a few apt distinctions, but we shall not
pursue the matter further. Austin was a member of
a long line of thinkers who emphasized the "will"
element in lawmaking. Let us now turn to a natural law theorist, St.
Thomas Aquinas. His tradition emphasizes the "reason" element. The
heart of his position is this:

> As Augustine says, that which is not just seems to be no law at all. Hence the force
> of a law depends on the extent of its justice.... Every human law has just so
> much of the nature of law as it is derived from the law of nature. But if in any
> point it departs from the law of nature, it is no longer a law but a perversion of
> law. (*Summa Theologiae*, I–II, q. 95) [9]

Clearly, Austin would have found this statement as offensive as Blackstone's.

A law, according to Aquinas, is "an ordinance of reason for the common good, promulgated by him who has the care of the community." This
general definition is meant to apply to four kinds of law: eternal, divine,
natural, and human (positive). Eternal law is God's law for the governance
of the universe, in the whole and in its parts; divine law directs human
beings to their supernatural end (the vision of God), while natural law
directs them to their earthly goal (happiness). Human law governs human
beings as members of the particular communities to which they belong.
Our focus is on the third and fourth kinds of law.

We can immediately note that for Aquinas, positive laws have a *coercive
power,* that is, they are backed up by sanctions. This is apparently contained in the notion of having "the care of the community." It brings
out the difference between offering advice on how social and personal
ends are to be attained and legislating on these ends. Thus a way is
provided for distinguishing between morality and the laws of a society,
though they are related. But in contrast to a positivistic view, it is not
this coercive backing which characterizes the laws as laws, according to
Aquinas. Laws possess their *directive power,* their authority to govern
conduct, insofar as they are gounded on reason. It is in virtue of this
that the pronouncements of the lawmaking agency impose obligations
and exist as valid laws in the society.

This grounding of laws on reason has two aspects, and for convenience
of exposition we shall consider them separately, although Aquinas would
not admit to a hard and fast distinction between them. Although he
would agree with Austin that laws are in some sense willed or commanded, basic to his theory is a crucial distinction (which Austin's

---

[9] *Basic Writings of St. Thomas Aquinas,* Anton C. Pegis, ed. (New York: Random
House, 1954), Vol. II, 784.

analysis does not allow for) between the rational directing of conduct and arbitrary expressions of desire that something should be done or forborne. A nonarbitrary command is a purposive act of will. It aims at the achieving of an end, and it is a function of reason to supply *directions,* or plans, toward ends. Lawmaking is itself a purposive activity in which directions, laws, are issued for the achievement of ends that people have as social beings and as members of particular communities. In framing laws the rational lawmaker will quite properly take into account the given social, economic, and historical circumstances. Legal systems, therefore, will to some extent differ in content and also change over time.

This aspect of Aquinas' theory is of the first importance, for it provides a theoretical basis for one kind of rational critique of lawmaking. It insists that human laws are means to ends and that they should be reasonable means to those ends. Whether a purported law has the "force of law" depends on its being a reasonable direction toward the attainment of a given end. Contemporary nonthomist exponents of natural law, such as Lon Fuller and Philip Selznick, also stress this point. As Selznick says, it is the function of legal scholarship to "reduce the arbitrariness" in positive law.

One of the criticisms that has been leveled at this aspect of Aquinas' theory is that it fails to explain why laws have the authority of obligations. For lawmaking, on this theory, involves what Immanuel Kant called "hypothetical imperatives." When the lawmaker issues his directive to do A, he is presupposing the validity of a hypothetical imperative of the form "If you wish to achieve end E, then you ought to (must) do A" or, perhaps, "If you wish to achieve E, then A is the best thing to do." Clearly, such hypothetical imperatives do not give rise to obligations. We can see this by considering the hypothetical imperative "If you wish to fix the kitchen sink, then you ought to (must) use a wrench." Even if it is assumed that one does wish to fix the sink, the consequent ("You ought to use a wrench") hardly amounts to an obligation to use a wrench. Laws, it is argued, are in exactly the same case.

Aquinas' reply to this objection ultimately rests on his conception of the ends to which laws are directed. This brings us to the second aspect of the grounding of laws on reason. It invokes the concepts of the common good—a law is "an ordinance of reason for the common good"— natural law and justice. This part of his theory is highly controversial.

As we saw above, according to Aquinas, lawmaking is a purposive activity. Its basis is the fact that humans are goal-oriented. It is natural for creatures to seek ends, and each kind of animate being has inclinations toward ends that are appropriate to its nature or essence. The fixing of the essences of things, and of the inclinations of creatures toward ends that complete their nature, is an aspect of the divine governance of the universe, i.e., eternal law. *Natural law,* in the traditional Thomist view, is "the participation of the eternal law in the rational creature." Just as it is a function of reason to supply directions for achieving ends, it is also a function of reason—without any divine assistance —to apprehend those ends that are appropriate to human nature. As such, these ends are apprehended as proper objects of pursuit, i.e., as goods. The principle underlying this operation of reason is: "Good is to be done and pursued; evil is to be avoided." Aquinas calls this the "first precept" of natural law. In the case of the lawmaker, who has the care of the community, the precept might well be formulated: the common good is to be done and pursued; what is bad for the community is to be avoided. Because the common good, for Aquinas, is the province of legal justice, a purported positive law that is not in conformity with natural law, justice, and the common good is to that extent "no longer a law, but a perversion of law." Enforcement of an unjust law is violence perpetrated against the citizen.

What gives content to the natural law is the rational apprehension of the essence of man and the human good. Aquinas develops this along Aristotelian lines. Man is by nature a social animal: he desires to live a life in common with other men, and he satisfies his needs and wants only in cooperative enterprise with others. One, therefore, ought to cooperate with others for one's own good as well as theirs. The first precept of natural law could, in fact, be formulated in this way. Now, social living has certain prerequisites whose fulfillment makes it possible. It requires, for example, that we should not harm our neighbors, which implies a prohibition against murder and theft. (This does not mean that it is necessarily contrary to natural law to kill in self-defense.) It requires the institutionalization of marriage and family life, hedged about with various prohibitions and responsibilities. It requires some mode of education as a way of initiating the young into society. This list could easily be extended, in the spirit of Aquinas, by following the tables of "basic needs" put forth by contemporary social scientists.

Such institutions, duties, and prohibitions are principles of natural law. Natural law, so conceived, should be distinguished from laws of nature of the sort that scientists seek to discover; namely, statements of uniform occurrence. The term, however, is ambiguous, and writers who use the language of natural law theory often switch without warning from one sense to the other. Aquinas wishes to maintain, on the one hand, that natural law can be violated (which would be impossible if the term referred to uniform occurrences); and, on the other hand, that there is a close connection between natural law and what man *is*—human nature. Because natural law contains prescriptions of what ought or ought not to be done, he has been criticized for illegitimately deriving normative propositions from factual propositions about human nature; it is held to be fallacious to deduce statements of what ought to be solely from statements of what is the case, or to infer judgments of value from judgments of fact.

Whether there really is a fallacy here is much debated.[10] Some contemporary moral philosophers have denied a sharp division between normative and factual judgments. Among legal philosophers, some of Aquinas' recent followers [11] think that there is a "blending" of what is and what ought to be; and Fuller (a nonthomist natural law theorist), in his early book *The Law in Quest of Itself* (1940), holds that we should "tolerate a confusion" between the two.

It is precisely this that is denied by the legal positivist's dictum "the existence of law is one thing; its merit or demerit is another." If fact and value, or Is and Ought, somehow merge, how then can we conceptually distinguish the law that is from the law that ought to be? Far from providing a way of evaluating the law, argues the positivist, this confusion actually *prevents* its evaluation. The natural law theorist, it would seem, is in danger of falling into a position which holds that the laws that prevail in a society have, by the very fact that they prevail, a certain degree of "moral oughtness" attached to them.

We will be in a better position to see whether Aquinas can escape this danger after examining a few more details of his theory. Toward the end of this chapter we shall also specifically consider the position of Selznick, who refuses to distinguish sharply between law and good law.

LAW AND MORALITY   The principles of natural law are a meeting ground for law and morality. They are binding in every society and their enforcement is required in every society. We may therefore say that a necessary condition for the existence of a legal system in the society is that the laws should contain at least the *minimum content* provided by these principles. This view has received sympathetic appreciation from Hart, who is a positivist of sorts, in his important book *The Concept of Law*.[12] He calls this the "core of good sense" in the doctrine of natural law, but his interpretation of it differs from that of Aquinas.

10 See Chapter Six of William Frankena's *Ethics*, 2nd ed., in this series.

11 See, for example, Heinrich Rommen, *The Natural Law*, trans. T. Hanley (St. Louis: B. Herder, 1947).

12 H. L. A. Hart, *The Concept of Law* (Oxford: Clarendon Press, 1961), pp. 189–95. See also the discussion of "jural postulates" in Roscoe Pound, *Outlines of Lectures on Jurisprudence*, 5th ed. (Cambridge: Harvard University Press, 1943), pp. 168–84.

In a discussion reminiscent of Hume's treatment of justice, Hart points out various facts about human nature that make necessary some of the the rules of social morality and law: men are vulnerable and liable to harm; they are approximately equal in intellectual and physical abilities; they are not completely selfish but have limited good will toward others; and they are limited in their powers of foresight and self-control. Finally, the resources that men need or desire are relatively scarce. Given these facts, if men are to live in society, they require rules that provide for the protection of the person and property, and that guarantee a degree of mutual forbearance and respect for the interests of others. Such rules are "fundamental" to a legal system in that without them there would be no point in having any other rules at all. In this way Hart dissociates himself from the thesis maintained by some positivists that "law may have any content." He would agree, however, that the presence of such rules in a society does not exclude the presence of laws that are bad or unjust.

Hart, then, also dissociates his position from Aquinas'. First of all, the necessity of the rules that comprise the minimum content of a legal system is dependent upon the prior assumption that *survival in proximity with others* is one of the aims that men have. Society, as Hart says, is not a "suicide club." This assumption, which is admittedly reflected in the way we think and talk about the human world, is a much more modest assumption than that of Aquinas, which holds that men are naturally inclined toward the human good, that is, toward ends that fulfill the human essence. It seems to me that, for Hart, the rules in question merely have the status of hypothetical imperatives: if men wish to survive in groups, they must have such and such rules. But for Aquinas, these rules have a more compelling status.

Second, contrary to what appears to be Aquinas' view, these rules are neither self-evident nor deducible from self-evident truths about human nature. The particular facts about human nature and the condition of relative scarcity are so obvious as to deserve to be called "truisms," according to Hart. But he insists that there is no necessity in them. Rather, these facts are contingent and are possibly subject to change. If, as is logically conceivable, there were a superabundance of commodities, there might be no recognition of private property and no prohibition against theft. Other changes in the minimum content of the laws of a society might also follow if there should be marked changes in human vulnerability, limited good will, etc. The minimal overlap between law and morality is, if necessary, merely "contingently necessary." Hart, therefore, would not agree that the principles of natural law are self-evident or that they are analytically contained in the concept of the existence of a legal system in a society.

On the last point, I think, Aquinas has a plausible reply. The concept of the existence of a legal system in a society, he could argue, is a concept that has developed within a framework of fairly specific ideas about man and his environment. Regarding *this* concept, the inclusion of the principles of natural law in the laws of a society is a matter of necessity in a stronger sense than Hart's; that is to say, it concerns the conditions for the application of the concept of a legal system. If human nature should change and men should become angels or beasts, our concept of law would simply not apply to them.

In the final analysis, Aquinas' disagreement with Hart turns on his theory of the essence of man, an essence fixed by the "participation of the eternal law in the rational creature." It is precisely this doctrine of a fixed human nature, with its theological underpinnings, that has proved a stumbling block to contemporary acceptance of natural law theory, in the words of the nonthomist natural law theorist A. P. d'Entrèves.[13] But Philip Selznick, also a nonthomist, holds that we should not overlook the "psychic unity" of mankind and the existence of cross-cultural universals. Social-scientific research may yet reveal to us what human nature is, according to Selznick, and it would be a piece of dogmatism to maintain otherwise. Principles of natural law, on this position, should be viewed as hypotheses that are open to revision as research progresses.[14] Some contemporary thomists are also sympathetic to this idea. It is not clear to me, however, how far it can be made compatible with Aquinas' doctrine of natural law and human nature, which is a doctrine that is really presented *within* a definite theological-ethical framework.

Aquinas' treatment of the process of lawmaking can be only briefly considered. As we saw, the laws of a society will include the principles of natural law. They will also include laws which, though not in themselves self-evident, can be deductively derived from the principles. Such laws have "some force from the natural law" and are, as it were, reenacted by the lawmaker. Another mode of derivation mentioned by Aquinas is that of "determination," in which the lawmaker fills in the gaps in the natural law. Thus, a principle of natural law forbids deception, but it is the task of the lawmaker to determine—to specify—the penalty for using the mails for fraudulent purposes, for example.

These two modes of derivation, however, do not really exhaust Aquinas' treatment. Laws are directions for achieving the common good, and most laws—especially in the modern state—cannot be derived from principles of natural law either by deduction or by determination. Rather, they represent the practical judgment of the lawmaker as to how the

---

[13] "The Case for Natural Law Re-examined," *Natural Law Forum,* 1 (1956), 27–46.
[14] "Sociology and Natural Law," *Natural Law Forum,* 6 (1961), 84–104.

common good can be promoted in the given circumstances. Such laws cannot in any sense be said to exist prior to their enactment. They are as much products of legislative will as of rational purpose.

We may now take up the question that we earlier postponed; namely, whether or not Aquinas is in danger of falling into a position which holds that whatever the lawmaker enacts is the law—the law is the law—and that some degree of "moral oughtness" attaches to the prevailing laws. It seems to me that if there is a danger here it is not a danger that results from any blending of the law that is with the law that ought to be. Nor is it peculiar to Aquinas' theory.

Aquinas is quite explicit on the matter. He lists the ways in which a purported law may be unjust and hence contrary to natural law: it may aim at the lawmaker's private good rather than the common good, it may aim at the common good but its burdens may be unfairly imposed, or it may exceed the constitutional or customary authority of the lawmaker to enact it into law. An unjust purported law is "violence rather than law" and there is no obligation to obey it except perhaps to avoid "scandal or disturbance."

Still, the above-mentioned danger arises because the judgment of the citizen may be opposed to the judgment of the lawmaker as to whether some enactment promotes the common good or is in fact unjust. Both judgments are fallible. Shall we therefore say that it is the citizen's judgment which must give way, that he must obey the law?

The dilemma here is not so much Aquinas'—his theoretical position is clear enough—as it is that of the conscientious citizen who must weigh obedience to what he believes is an unjust enactment against the harms that might result from disobedience.[15] But Aquinas also admits that in estimating these harms one must also take into account the fact that the enactment was made under the color of law and that any disobedience to it undermines the authority of laws. (Aquinas, like Austin, has a fear of anarchy.) One reason for compliance is that the enactment is an enactment of the lawmaker, and to this extent Aquinas would appear to assign "moral oughtness" to it.

We shall take leave of Aquinas with a final point. It is his precept that the lawmaker should pursue the common good. But what is the common good, and how shall we discover it? The problem of determining the common good or the public interest, as it is now called, is exacerbated in modern societies. There are a variety of groups whose interests are often in conflict. What is needed is a way of adjusting conflicting interests, and Aquinas does not give us much help on this score. Resort to natural inclinations, or needs and wants, does not seem to be enough. These are

15 For a discussion of the basis of political obligation, see Joel Feinberg, *Social Philosophy,* in this series.

also frequently in conflict, and a method of adjustment is required. I do not mean to suggest that this problem is insuperable. Nor is it exclusive to theorists who analyze the nature of law in terms of the common good. It must be faced by anyone who believes that the laws ought to promote the good of man and society.

THE PREDICTION THEORY: HOLMES

Aquinas' theory, as we have seen, brings into play a grand metaphysical structure. Let us now turn to a writer whose starting point seems to be at the opposite extreme: Oliver Wendell Holmes, Jr., one of the great Justices of the U.S. Supreme Court. His essay "The Path of the Law" is probably the most influential essay in American legal thought. His position is popularly called the *bad man* or *prediction* theory of law.

Holmes would have endorsed Austin's statement that the existence of law is one thing, its merit or demerit another. As a result of the overlap in phraseology—both speak of rights, duties, malice, intent, negligence, etc.—he found a confusion between moral and legal concepts at every turn in traditional doctrine. The law is not a "brooding omnipresence in the sky." Nor is it coextensive with any system of ethics. If one wishes to know what the laws of a society are one must, according to Holmes, approach the question from the perspective of the bad man.

The bad man does not give two straws for morality but he, no less than the good man, wishes to avoid an encounter with the law. When he asks his lawyer whether some contemplated action is legal, what he wants to know is how public power is going to affect him. In answering this question, according to Holmes, the lawyer's job is one of prediction. A legal duty, says Holmes, is "nothing but a prediction that if a man does or omits certain things he will be made to suffer in this or that way by judgment of the court—and so of a legal right." [16] Laws are "prophecies of what the courts will do in fact." The kind of prophecy intended by Holmes is a generalized prediction of judicial judgments in a given type of case and not, as some later American "legal realists" held, a prediction of the decision of some particular judge in a specific case.

This is a bracing view. Just as Austin washed the law with logical acid, Holmes bathes it in cynical acid. Holmes does not deny that moral conceptions influence the growth of the law. One of his major contributions to legal philosophy, in fact, is that judicial decision making frequently involves value judgments. These are often unarticulated major premises which are hidden from sight by the logical form into which the judge's opinion is cast. The prediction theory, however, is not a theory of the

16 O. W. Holmes, Jr., "The Path of the Law," *Harvard Law Rev.*, 10 (1897), 458.

development of law but of the "limits" of law, a theory of what are the laws of a society.

This theory, I think, has the merit of providing one very illuminating way to look at law, but it cannot stand as a general theory (if Holmes really meant it as such). A serious difficulty is that in adopting the perspective of the potential litigant, it leaves out the perspective of the judge. The judge is surely not trying to predict what he or other judges will decide when he asks himself what the law is on the issue of the case. It might be replied that the judge is trying to predict what higher courts would decide if his judgment should be appealed. But this holds no water because the judge in question might be a member (or the sole member) of the highest appellate court. Moreover, a legal system need not provide for appeals.

An important question that Holmes does not take up is whence the courts derive their authority. What is it that constitutes courts as jural agents and the decisions of judges as jural acts? A standard way of answering this is by reference to power-delegating laws or laws of competence. To interpret these as predictions of the judgments of courts would seem to involve a circularity. It might be possible to handle this with some elaborate version of the behavioral approach mentioned in the preceding chapter, but I think it will have to include statements about the behavior of others besides judges.

One problem with Holmes' theory is that it is court-centered, and does not seem to apply to legal systems without courts. This consideration led some of Holmes' "realist" followers to broaden the theory to cover any law-enforcing or law-applying officials. But, as Hermann Kantorowicz points out, what these officials enforce or apply are laws and not predictions about each other's judgments or behavior.[17] This should not be understood to mean that the laws are always ready-made and waiting to be enforced or applied. Professor Fuller demolishes any such idea in his *Anatomy of the Law,* and both Holmes and Kantorowicz would agree with him.

Kantorowicz' point, however, is well-taken and can be extended to show that the court-centered, or even official-centered, view also distorts the perspective of the ordinary member of society in relation to laws. Consider the game of baseball. It has rules which the players know and follow. It would be grossly misleading to say that these rules are simply generalized predictions of what umpires would decide. So also for the laws of a society. Both ordinary citizens and judges *use* laws as guides to action. Of course, the law is a much more serious and open-ended affair than baseball, and the decisions of judges and other officials have high visibility for the citizen: judges and officials are participants in the lawmaking process. The point nevertheless stands, and it serves us as a transition to

17 "Some Rationalism about Realism," *Yale Law Journal,* 43 (1934), 1240–52.

the theory of another legal positivist, Hans Kelsen. Kelsen is probably the most influential twentieth-century legal theorist, particularly on the Continent and in Latin America.

LAWS AS NORMS:
KELSEN

It should be noticed that on the prediction theory laws are descriptive statements. The deontic, or "ought," element has entirely dropped out. This is completely unacceptable to Kelsen, for laws, he maintains, are *norms.* Their meaning cannot be expressed without using normative language, particularly the term "ought." But this term does not refer to a moral ought.

Kelsen calls his theory a *pure* theory of law.[18] This can be explained by recalling our description of the hypothetical legal system of the South Sea Islanders. Kelsen would first of all insist that our account should be kept clear of any ideological or ethical bias (as is contained in Aquinas' doctrine of natural law, for example). Kelsen thus endorses Austin's dictum on the existence of law. Second, he would insist that we should not confuse our statements of what are the laws with descriptive statements about the behavior of either officials or nonofficials. One of the principal aims of the pure theory is to provide the conceptual tools for "representing" the laws of a society in a way that expresses their jural character and actual content and also displays their interconnections within the system.

There are many kinds of systems of norms. A legal order, according to Kelsen, is a normative system which uses coercive techniques to secure compliance. From this Kelsen draws the conclusion—to which I do not think he is entitled—that a statement representing the content of a law must represent it as sanction-stipulating. The canonical form of such statements is a hypothetical: If it is determined by competent authority that such and such (e.g., a particular act) has occurred, then a competent authority ought to impose this or that sanction (e.g., a jail sentence, an order to pay a creditor).[19] The "ought" is essential here, and according to Kelsen (especially in his recent writings) it can mean "must," "may," or "is authorized."

Now it is important to notice that the statements by which *we*

---

[18] Kelsen's writings are voluminous. His main works in English translation are *The Pure Theory of Law,* trans. M. Knight (Berkeley: University of California Press, 1967) and *General Theory of Law and State,* trans. A. Wedberg (Cambridge: Harvard University Press, 1946).

[19] In order to facilitate our representation we are permitted to speak in the usual way, that (for example) the law forbids smoking in the subway. But the "real content" can only be expressed in the canonical form, which tells a law-applying official what he ought to do.

represent the laws of the island society are *not* laws ("legal norms"). These statements are not prescriptions, but reports that may be true or false. It is one of Kelsen's intriguing theses, which we cannot examine here, that the hypothetical statements which represent laws must employ a deontic term, but that the "ought" in the consequent is used descriptively, not normatively. Our statements, however, by no means describe the way people behave in the society although, as we shall see shortly, their truth does presuppose some descriptions of this sort.

In order to represent the laws we first have to identify them. This in turn requires, on Kelsen's view, that we should be able to identify acts of lawmaking. His slogan is that "all law is positive law," which means for him that laws are created and annulled by *acts of will,* a doctrine which seems to have its origins in a Kantian separation of the realms of Is and Ought and a sharp distinction between cognition and volition. These acts of will are not Austinian commands, which are expressions of desire. When the absolute monarch, King Rex, in our island society issues his command that everyone should take a bath on Saturday nights, his *wanting* them to do this is irrelevant to its status as law. I think this is correct. But it also seems to me that the doctrine that laws are created by acts of will is subject to the kinds of criticism that Maine and Fuller advance against the command theory. In any event, if this doctrine is plausible in Rex's case, it is implausible in the case of a multimembered legislature, as Axel Hägerström points out.[20] At best, Hägerström's objection is only partially mitigated by another Kelsenian thesis; namely, that laws are not the acts of will themselves but, rather, the "objective meaning" of such acts. This thesis is the key to identifying acts of lawmaking and the laws of the society.

Suppose both King Rex and John, who is a member of the island community, want everyone to take a bath on Saturday nights and each issues the declaration: "Everyone should take a bath on Saturday nights!" In Kelsen's terms their declarations are identical in "subjective meaning," but only Rex's has an "objective meaning" which is established as a law, for Rex's declaration is in consonance with another law which states that the commands of Rex are valid (i.e., binding) laws.

This, of course, is a highly simplified model of lawmaking, but it illustrates Kelsen's position that laws regulate the creation of laws. A law, as he puts it, derives its *validity* from another law (or laws). The laws of a legal system thus form a hierarchical structure, and the validity of a lower legal norm is justified by appeal to a higher legal norm, either because the content of the former conforms to the latter or because the creation of the former is authorized by the latter. This aspect of Kelsen's

[20] *Inquiries into the Nature of Law and Morals,* trans. C. D. Broad (Stockholm: Almquist and Wiksell, 1953), passim.

theory raises many intricate points which we cannot go into here, but what is important for us is his view that the validity of a law can only be derived from another law which is itself a valid law. Our representation of the laws of the society must also reflect this fact. There is a correspondence between the conditions for the validity of a law and the criteria for identifying law-creating acts of will. Laws function as "schemes of interpretation" for such identifications. Legal norms cannot be identified unless we already have (what might be called) a normative perspective.

The above considerations lead to the focal point of Kelsen's theory and its most characteristic doctrine. In tracing back the validity of one law to that of another, we ultimately come to the law from which the validity of all the others of the given system is derived. This is the Basic Norm (*Grundnorm*) of the system. It states, for example, that King Rex should be obeyed, or that laws made in conformity with procedures for lawmaking as specified in the constitution are valid. The Basic Norm of a system, however, is not itself a positive law; indeed it might never be expressed by those who live under the system. Its validity is *presupposed* in the making of laws and in identifying acts of will as law-creating acts; it supplies the normative perspective. With the Basic Norm we reach the limits of legal positivism. One might, of course, attempt to derive the validity of the Basic Norm of a system from a moral or ideological norm of some sort (e.g., a principle of legitimacy) but Kelsen refuses to take this step. Once we reach the Basic Norm we have all that is necessary for the representation of the laws of a society, and Kelsen is not disturbed by the apparent paradox that the existence of laws presupposes the existence of law.

There is one more point to consider before we turn to some critical comment. We saw that according to the pure theory the laws of a society should not be identified with statements about the way people behave. The fact that all the Islanders take a bath on Saturday nights does not imply that there is a law to this effect. Nor, on the other hand, would their failure to take a bath show that there is no law that requires bathing. When behavior conforms to a law (irrespective of the motive for such conformance), the law is said by Kelsen to be "effective." Now when we assert that a system of valid laws exists in a society, a necessary condition of the truth of the assertion is that the laws are *by and large* effective. The laws that exist in the territory of Russia are Soviet laws and not the laws of czarist Russia, although the latter were once effective there. A group of laws may lose validity by ceasing to be effective. The truth of statements representing the laws of a society therefore presupposes certain descriptions of the behavior of its members (strictly speaking, the behavior of officials). Nevertheless, according to Kelsen, what confers validity upon the laws is not their effectiveness. Validity is ultimately derived from the Basic Norm of the given system.

Kelsen provides many important insights and original ideas. Nevertheless his theory suffers from internal difficulties.

Consider the point just mentioned: that the validity of the laws of a system is established by reference to its Basic Norm. It seems to me that Kelsen is moving in a circle. For the Basic Norm is discovered in our representation of the system by tracing back through the valid laws to the presupposed norm from which they all derive their validity. (And what really guarantees that there is one norm that does the job?) But this process assumes that we can already tell what the valid laws are independently of the Basic Norm.

The meaning of "valid law" is also problematic. Although Kelsen explicitly rejects any so-called "recognition theory," it is not clear that he entirely escapes one at some level. A recognition theory holds that the valid laws are norms that are recognized or accepted as *binding* by those who are subject to them. Now, in a recent article Kelsen maintains that a Basic Norm is presupposed by anyone who considers a particular effective coercive order to be a system of valid laws. By this he means that when the members or officials of the society consider the particular order to be a system of binding norms, they are presupposing the validity of some Basic Norm.[21] (There is no necessity that these individuals should view the effective coercive order as a legal system; they can instead view it as a plain "gunman writ large" situation; there need be no difference for them between the tax collector and a bandit. This is contrary to Austin's view. According to Austin, given a habit of obedience—i.e., effective commands—we have a legal system and legal obligations.) Apparently, then, Kelsen does employ something like the notion of "recognition"—for these individuals to consider a law to be valid is the same as their considering it binding on them—and his complaint against the recognition theory is only that it leaves out the Basic Norm. It seems that Kelsen cannot completely escape a recognition theory at some level, especially because the starting point for giving a representation of a legal system is its valid laws, as we saw above.

But this conclusion raises the question of whether or not the doctrine

[21] Hans Kelsen, "On the Pure Theory of Law," *Israel Law Rev.*, 1 (1966), 1–7. Contrary to what he appears to say elsewhere, in this article Kelsen denies that the Basic Norm is also a presupposition of the legal scientist who is constructing a representation of a particular system. For the legal scientist, the Basic Norm serves only an epistemological function; that is, as a device for interpreting a coercive order as a system of valid laws. It is the members or officials of the society who presuppose the Basic Norm (i.e., presuppose its validity) when they regard the order as a system of norms which are binding upon them. This topic merits further research. Kelsen's position should be compared with that of Hart on the internal and external points of view, discussed later in the chapter.

of the Basic Norm is superfluous. Does the legal scientist really need a normative perspective in order to give a representation of the valid laws of a system, even if it only serves an "epistemological function"?

Professor Alf Ross, who seems to hold what Kelsen would call a recognition theory, argues this point. Ross uses the game of chess as an example. It is quite unnecessary to think that there is some Basic Norm of chess that either we or the players presuppose in order to give a representation of the valid rules of chess. Ross concedes that *behavioral* considerations alone are insufficient: if no one ever opens with a rook's pawn, that would not show that there is a rule that forbids it. We must also take into account a *psychological* factor. We need to know the "spiritual life" of the players, what they believe or experience as binding upon them. So also with law, except that the relevant individuals are judges (or law-applying officials). A valid system of legal norms in a given territory is comprised of "the norms which actually are operative in the mind of the judge, because they are felt by him to be socially binding and therefore obeyed." [22] Reference to a Basic Norm, according to Ross, only distorts the relationship between the idea of a norm and social reality (i.e., patterns of behavior).

The notion of what is "felt" to be binding seems somewhat obscure to me. Instead of analyzing it further, however, let us turn to the positivistic position of H. L. A. Hart, who freshly reworks many of the insights of Kelsen and Ross.

RULES:
H. L. A. HART

Hart's book *The Concept of Law* is one of the truly elegant works in legal philosophy. Its aim is to give an account of the central features of legal systems in terms of which their other features may be understood, in order to bring out the complex relationships of legal systems to other types of social institution. For this we need the idea of a *rule*. Rules are central to legal systems and to other types of institutions. As Hart's extensive critique shows, neither orders backed by threats nor predictions of behavior do the job of explaining what rules are. Basic to Hart's analysis of legal validity and the existence of a legal system is his distinction between *internal* and *external* points of view regarding rules.

Hart begins by asking what it is for a society or group to have a rule. This question he answers in terms of the acceptance of the rule. "Acceptance" does not mean moral approval or a feeling of being bound. A rule (e.g., "A man must take off his hat on entering a church") sets up a standard of conduct. A group of persons cannot be said to have accepted

22 Alf Ross, *On Law and Justice* (London: Stevens and Sons, Ltd., 1958), p. 35.

a rule merely when the standard is generally complied with, for this would amount to viewing the rule purely from an external perspective. It must also be the case that a deviation from the standard is generally taken by the group as a fault open to criticism and as a good enough reason for making a criticism. To have such an "internal point of view" or "reflective critical attitude" regarding the conduct specified by the standard (the conduct itself being the "external" aspect of the rule) is to accept the rule. When an observer of the group makes a statement to the effect that a given rule exists in it, this means both that the members generally comply with the particular standard and that the members have adopted an internal point of view regarding it. The motives for the acceptance of a rule may vary from member to member. Finally, according to Hart, a rule will be considered as imposing an *obligation* when the general demand for conformity to its standard is insistent and the social pressure brought to bear on those who deviate or threaten to deviate is great.[23]

Now Hart concedes that it is possible for a society to have a set of rules comprised only of the kind just mentioned. Such a social structure is said to be a regime of *primary* rules of obligation. It works successfully only so long as the community is closely knit and in a stable environment. Under other conditions this kind of regime will prove defective in three ways. (1) Uncertainty: doubts will arise as to what the rules are or as to their precise scope. (2) Static character: the only mode of change in the rules will be the slow processes of growth and decay. (3) Inefficiency: the rules will be maintained only by diffuse social pressure and there will be no way of settling with finality whether or not a rule has been violated.

These defects, says Hart, may be remedied by the introduction of *secondary* rules. For the first, a *rule of recognition* may be adopted, which specifies some characteristic in terms of which the primary rules may be authoritatively identified. This rule may amount to no more than specifying a list of primary rules carved on a public monument. Or it may actually be a complex set of rules such as is found in modern societies (e.g., "What the Queen in Parliament enacts is law"). The second defect may be remedied by the adoption of *rules of change,* which provide for deliberate alteration of primary rules, generally by designating individuals who have the authority under certain conditions to initiate changes. Legislative enactment and repeal are to be understood in terms of such rules rather than in terms of orders backed by threats. Obviously, there is a close connection between such rules and rules of recognition. Finally, inefficiency may be remedied by introducing *rules of adjudication,* which authorize individuals to determine, usually according to a specified

23 *Quaere:* If the acceptance of a rule is based on fear, aren't we at the level of "being obliged" rather than at that of obligation? Shouldn't there be some moral ground for the acceptance?

procedure, when a primary rule has been violated and to provide for its enforcement. Legal history, says Hart, suggests that this third kind of secondary rule tends to be adopted before the other two.

With the above account, Hart has described the steps from the "pre-legal into the legal world." Law is the *union of primary and secondary rules.* (The reader will have already noticed the parallelism between Hart's rules of change and adjudication and three of our jural agencies.) Because the introduction of secondary rules may take place in a gradual and partial manner, it would seem that the existence of a legal system can be a matter of degree. I think that Hart clearly avoids the kind of criticism that Maine made of Austin and that applies also to Kelsen.

There are, however, some difficulties to be noted. Secondary rules are characterized in several ways by Hart. Thus in some places any non-mandatory rule (for example, a rule providing for testamentary succession) seems accounted a secondary rule. But what is crucial about the rules of recognition, change, and adjudication is that they are rules *about* rules, as Hart says. In any case, the difficulty is that it is not at all clear that Hart's initial characterization of rules and their existence applies to secondary rules. It is hard to see how these rules set up standards of conduct and, therefore, what would be the adoption of an internal point of view regarding them.

The concept of valid law is explained by Hart with reference to the secondary rules of a system and especially its ultimate rule of recognition. A primary rule of obligation is a valid law of a given system if it conforms to a rule of recognition. But here it should be noticed that there is a discontinuity between Hart's initial characterization of primary rules of obligation and his position on the existence of rules of recognition, change, and adjudication. In the former case the individuals whose acceptance was held necessary are those who are subject to the rules; in the latter case the essentially relevant individuals are the (law-applying) officials of the system. It turns out, therefore, that the general membership of the society need not have an internal point of view regarding a primary rule of obligation for it to be a valid law; it need only conform to a rule of recognition. In this event, it is not clear in what sense such a rule imposes an obligation, except in that it is a rule set by political superiors (officials) to inferiors, as Austin would say.

Two conditions must be satisfied for a legal system to exist in a society, according to Hart. First, the valid laws must be obeyed by the bulk of the membership. This apparently means that they must be *effective* in Kelsen's behavioral sense of the term. The second condition is that the rules of recognition, change, and adjudication must be accepted by the officials. But who are the officials? It seems circular to say that the officials are those who are empowered by rules that exist as rules because they are recognized by the officials. In order to get around this difficulty it appears that Hart would indirectly have to reinstate something like Austin's "habit of obedience." The officials are those individuals whom the bulk of the membership habitually obey. It is not just the laws that are obeyed.

Hart's treatment of the ultimate rule of recognition should be compared with Kelsen's doctrine of the Basic Norm. The Basic Norm, in Kelsen's view, must be presumed to be a valid law, for validity can follow only from validity. But according to Hart, it makes no sense to ask whether the ultimate standard for the validity of particular laws is itself a valid law. The ultimate rule of recognition of a system is not a valid law; its existence is a "matter of fact." Presumably, assertions to this effect are made from an external point of view: the ultimate rule of recognition is said to exist as the concordant "practice" of officials in identifying the laws of the society by reference to certain criteria (e.g., being listed among the rules carved on a monument). But how can a practice—what is merely *done*—be a rule? One must therefore add, I think, that the practice is somehow accepted as a standard of conduct. That a standard is accepted is a matter of fact. However, it is debatable whether the acceptance in this case can be reduced to the behavior of officials, which is what Hart apparently wishes to do. Ross, for one, would reject any such reduction.

I do not mean to suggest that the above-mentioned difficulties are in any way fatal to Hart's theory. On the contrary, it seems to me that his theory is highly illuminating, and it constitutes a positivistic approach to law which successfully avoids many of the rather serious difficulties and even obscurities that other positivists end up in. My main question about Hart's theory, however, is whether it covers the whole ground or needs supplementation of a major sort.

We have already encountered Hart's view that the "contingently necessary" connection between law and morality does not go counter to Austin's distinction between the existence and merits of a law. This is a distinction which Hart, like the other positivists, accepts. One issue we have not considered is whether Fuller's criticism of Austin's command theory has any force against Hart. When this criticism was first mentioned, I stated that it is not directed exclusively at Austin but is part of a broad attack on legal positivism. It is made in the name of a closer connection between law and morality than the positivists would admit. Let us now turn to Fuller's theory and see how this claim is developed.

FULLER'S CRITIQUE OF POSITIVISM

Fuller brings us back to the natural law tradition. The theory he defends, however, is nonthomist, and the theological-metaphysical structure is absent. Moreover, Fuller does not propose anything like Aquinas' standards for evaluating particular purported laws. He is more concerned with the overall workings of legal systems, and he stresses the difficulty of evaluating individual laws. His theory is one of "procedural" natural law and it is supposed to serve with near-equal neutrality a variety of opposed substantive aims. Two related themes affiliate Fuller with the natural law tradition: an interest in discovering principles of social order which the lawmaker must take into account if he is to be successful at his task, and a stress on the role of reason in the lawmaking process.[24]

Fuller begins his critique of legal positivism with these themes. He concedes that there is a purely arbitrary element in law. And he would concede, I think, that many rules have the status of law simply because they conform to stipulated procedures or rules of recognition. But this cannot be the whole story of what it takes to have a legal system. Homely examples are brought to bear on the point. A group of people are shipwrecked on an island, or a group of people go on an extended camping trip. It soon emerges that various individuals will have to be assigned certain tasks and that the conduct of the members will have to be regulated. Obviously, these processes of task assignment and regulation are purposive in character, and if we wish to understand them we have to see not only the element of fiat but also the role that reason plays in them. It is just this which the positivists' account of a legal system leaves out. They begin with a supposedly finished system, and make no place for the problems involved in "creating and managing" a legal system.[25] If a society were to suffer a devastating revolution and started to create its legal system anew, it would get little guidance from the legal positivist, Fuller argues.

Underlying Fuller's position is a concept of law (or lawmaking) as the *enterprise of subjecting human conduct to the governance of rules.*[26] Law is an "activity," and a legal system is the result of sustained purposive effort. Fuller finds that the legal enterprise faces pervasive problems. There is the problem of keeping the various institutions and official roles in accord with one another. And there is the problem of contending with the ambiguities and uncertainties that are introduced by the fact that legal institutions and rules serve a multiplicity of ends. Fuller demonstrates that it is no easy task to devise rules which will ensure that our laws or jural agencies do not work at cross-purposes. The issue also touches the operation of a single jural agency. Consider Hart's secondary rules of adjudication by which individuals are empowered to decide con-

[24] The theme of Fuller's earlier writings, that there is a "fusion" of Is and Ought, is hardly mentioned explicitly in his most recent works.

[25] The utilitarians (especially Bentham) were concerned with the "science of legislation," but they sharply distinguished it from their theory of the existence of law.

[26] Fuller, *The Morality of Law,* p. 106.

troversies over the violation of a primary rule. Clearly, the institution thereby created cannot properly perform its function unless the roles of judge, prosecutor, and defendant are kept separate. But it is not merely a question of whether the institution is going to be able to carry out its task well. Fuller would argue, I think, that unless appropriate rules for its functioning are devised, there is also a question (of degree, perhaps) of whether an agency for adjudication actually exists.

Now it might be thought that at least some of these problems can be easily remedied by introducing a precise chain of command into which the jural agencies and activities fit. All we need, it might be said, are precise criteria of legal validity, e.g., rules of recognition. The simplest cure would be to designate a King Rex as the font of the law. But as Fuller shows in his eight ways in which Rex can fail to make law, this might be no solution at all. If Rex pursues a policy of secret legislation, excessive retroactive legislation, etc., he will fail in the enterprise of subjecting conduct to the governance of rules. King Rex is only a figure of speech. Fuller shows that even more sophisticated remedies might fail.

There is much in the above that a positivist of Hart's variety can agree with. Hart also maintains that rules are essential to a legal system and that Rex will have failed to make laws if he has failed to make rules. But what Fuller is trying to establish is intended to cut below Hart and other legal positivists. The point of Fuller's figure of speech is this: there are conditions for successful lawmaking that cannot straightforwardly be written into the positive law, and these conditions have to be met even if they are not written into the positive law.

Fuller admittedly has great difficulty in formulating these conditions in other than very general terms. They are best brought out as contrasts to the eight ways of failure. Fuller characterizes these conditions as *the morality that makes law possible*. While Aquinas' theory centers around a morality "external" to the law, to which law must conform, Fuller's "legal morality" is *internal* to the law itself. It seems to me that there are difficulties in his characterization of the eightfold path to "legality." Before we consider them, a bit more should be said about Fuller's theory.

According to Fuller, a total failure with respect to any of the desiderata of "legal morality" does not simply result in a bad system of law but rather in no legal system at all. Total failure, however, will be extremely rare. Difficult questions arise concerning the jural status of a purported legal system when there is partial failure with respect to one or more of the eight conditions. Clearly, the desiderata are, at best, guidelines for constructing a legal system. It is difficult (as Fuller is aware) to apply any of the conditions in order to judge the legalness of an individual law. Fuller, in fact, is at pains to point out, for instance, that retroactive legislation, which we generally hold to be morally reprehensible, is sometimes required to cure faults in the system.

For these reasons Fuller's share in his exchange with Hart over the status of Nazi law is somewhat inconclusive.[27] Like a good positivist, Hart maintains that the instance under discussion was bad law, but law nonetheless. He would cure the evil with retroactive legislation. Fuller, on the other hand, maintains that this part of Nazi law was so defective in legal morality (because of *ad hoc* laws, secret laws, retroactive laws, etc.) that the given instance failed to achieve the status of law. However, even on his own terms, the issue is not easily settled. It seems to me that Fuller cannot entirely reject Austin's now-famous distinction when it comes to individual laws.

Let us now turn to Fuller's characterization of the conditions for lawmaking. Why do they constitute a "morality"? Fuller in fact distinguishes two moralities, a morality of duty and a morality of aspiration. Certain activities, he holds, are governed more by a morality of aspiration than a morality of duty. For example, the achieving of excellence in the arts is a matter of aspiration, and artistic failures are not derelictions of duty. Thus, wherever we have identifiable forms of sustained purpose, as in the professions and crafts, that can be pursued with different degrees of success, we have an "internal morality" coordinate with each of them. It is comprised of the conditions that must be met in order to achieve the enterprise's goal. Apparently because there is a legislative art that can be plied with varying degrees of success, Fuller holds that his legal morality is basically a morality of aspiration.

I find this explanation hard to accept, for it involves an overextension of the term "morality." It would seem strange to call the conditions for good golf-playing the "inner morality of golf" or the conditions for excellence in safe-cracking (a recognized profession) an "internal morality." Not all kinds of excellence are moral, so not all matters of aspiration involve a "morality of aspiration."

Interestingly, in his recent book *Anatomy of the Law*, Fuller usually refers to the conditions for success in the lawmaking enterprise as being "implicit laws" of lawmaking. Only rarely does he refer to them as a "legal morality." But I think that it is not incorrect to characterize them as *moral guidelines* for lawmakers and officials if they are to act in a fair and responsible fashion toward the members of a society. Fuller's legal morality is at least part of what is meant by the "rule of law" and the "just administration" of laws. Adherence to it will lessen arbitrary treat-

---

27 H. L. A. Hart, "Positivism and the Separation of Law and Morals," and Lon L. Fuller, "Positivism and Fidelity to Law—A Reply to Professor Hart," *Harvard Law Rev.*, 71 1958), 593–629 and 630–72.

ment of the public by lawmakers and law-appliers. The citizen is liable to suffer an injustice whenever laws are unclear or whenever administration of the law does not accord with the law as announced. It is doubtful, moreover, what the individual's "obligations" are in relation to the law or that there even are any laws which impose obligations on him, in such circumstances. I also think that it is not incorrect to characterize these guidelines as "internal" to the law, for they are derived from the nature of the enterprise of lawmaking, as Fuller defines it. In a moment we shall see how Selznick develops this point. I should like to add, however, that adherence to these guidelines does not entirely rule out the possibility of laws that are bad or unjust according to some substantive ("external") standard. Still, Fuller does show that there is a rather intricate connection between the questions of the existence of law and obligation.

LEGAL AUTHORITY:
SELZNICK

What puts Selznick in the natural law tradition is his refusal to make a sharp distinction between law and good law. Like Fuller, he presents a generic notion of law.[28] Law exists whenever a group (public or private) accepts rules as authoritative and where there are agencies whose ministrations with respect to the rules are accepted as authoritative. The legal element is the invocation of authority, not sanctions. The *ideal of legality* emerges where rational forms of social organization prevail. Following Max Weber, Selznick traces three kinds of legitimation of authority: traditional, charismatic, and rational-legal. In the third there is an attempt to exclude the arbitrary exercise of authority by subjecting it to the governance of rules that are designed to achieve the goals of the given institution. Legal authority, in a full sense, exists when authority itself is subject to restraints.

The ideal of legality, however, is not a pre-existent code of laws; nor is it identifiable with any code of laws any more than the ideal of sportsmanship is identifiable with the rules of any game. Rather, legality implies standards for the exercise of authority, and it requires that the lawmaker should "affirm reason," according to Selznick. It prescribes that close attention should be given to the relationship between means and ends, and that the desirability of ends should be clarified in the light of reason. By "reason" Selznick means what John Dewey calls "scientific intelligence." The findings of social science are not only indispensible to the rational lawmaker, they also have *legal* authority.

Selznick maintains that the legal ordering of a group (a society, an

---

[28] Philip Selznick, *Law, Society, and Industrial Justice* (New York: Russell Sage Foundation, 1969), pp. 3–34; "Sociology and Natural Law," *Natural Law Forum*, 6 (1961), 84–104.

industrial organization) develops out of a need for rational regulation. The ideal of legality therefore has a natural foundation and objective worth. We may say, I think, that the ideal of legality is "internal" to law. Given its function, a bad legal system is bad *as* a legal system. Selznick tries to show how his theory helps us in diagnosing cases of "legal pathology," breakdowns in the effort at effective governance. He grants that the positive laws of a society are those rules that are acted upon by institutions whose authority is accepted. (This appears to be a kind of recognition theory of legal validity.) To this extent his view is compatible with Austin's distinction between the existence and merits of a law. At the same time, Selznick maintains that a rule made in violation of the ideal of legality is less of a legal rule than one that conforms to legality. The former is not just bad law, it is inferior *as* law. Such a law does not command our full respect, and I think Selznick wants to say that the obligation it imposes is, in some way, incomplete.

Despite its merits, Selznick's argument seems to involve an equivocal use of the term "reason." Reason in the sense of scientific intelligence is not the same as the "formal rationality" of the third kind of legitimation of authority. The affirmation of reason (legality), according to Selznick, requires the lawmaker to be sensitive to the integrity of the human person as a free being and as a being whose interests deserve protection. But although a violation of legality in this respect might be arbitrary and unjust, it is not clear to me that it would violate reason either in the sense of scientific intelligence or in the sense of adherence to the rules of the system (formal rationality). Selznick, in effect, incorporates certain substantive values into his concept of reason. In this respect he is close to the classical thomist position.

Selznick and Fuller continue and develop the natural law tradition's emphasis on the role of reason in lawmaking and its view of a necessary connection between law and morality. The theories of both Selznick and Fuller also require, and to some extent already explicitly contain, elements of Hart's theory, particularly the idea of secondary rules and the idea of the acceptance of a rule. But the detailed working out of an extended theory, which combines the approaches of all three of these writers, has yet to be accomplished. Whether it can be worked out on a consistent basis remains to be seen.

CHAPTER THREE

The Limits
of Law

PROTECTED RIGHTS

One of the sharpest issues in contemporary legal philosophy concerns the permissible limits of legal compulsion. It is so notorious as to have acquired a name, the "enforcement of morals" controversy, for it takes its departure from a lecture of that title by the British judge Lord Patrick Devlin.[1] Much of the literature is centered around the use of the law to enforce standards of sexual conduct. But this is discussed in terms of broad principles about the legitimate uses of the law. At stake here is a normative question—not a conceptual or definitional question, such as concerned us in the preceding chapter.[2] What ends should the law promote, and what ends should it not promote? Are there spheres of activity with which it would be wrong for the law to interfere? It is this last and rather

[1] This lecture was reprinted as "Morals and the Criminal Law" in Devlin's book *The Enforcement of Morals* (London: Oxford University Press, 1965).

[2] It should be emphasized that a number of the writers we considered also supplied a positive rationale, a justification, for having a legal system or for having some laws: for example, laws arise from a natural need for regulation, laws provide certain necessary protections to persons and property, laws are means for promoting the common good.

negative issue which has been uppermost in the minds of the participants in the dispute.[3]

This is the very basic issue of authority and freedom. What does a society have the right to demand of its members in the way of affirmative action or restraint? And what ought to be reserved to the individual as subject to his own choice and decision? These questions are the traditional fare of ethics and political and social philosophy. In the modern state we can hardly avoid thinking of them in terms of the law, for most of our activities, even those of an intimate sort, come within its scope. Treatment of this issue inevitably leads to a consideration of the limits of law. Before we turn to some of the writers, a few general remarks are necessary to set the problem.

One is tempted to give a rather quick answer to the question of the degree of freedom that an individual ought to have: as much as possible. But as soon as we consider the concrete meaning of the concept of freedom in an organized social setting it becomes clear that this simple answer is not helpful. Freedom is a complex topic, and this is not the place for a detailed analysis.[4] It is sufficient for our purposes to indicate the sense of "freedom" that is implicit in the quick answer: Freedom is the ability to do whatever one wishes. In slightly expanded form, freedom is the ability to act in terms of one's interests, desires, and tastes; it is the ability to act in order to realize one's aims, whatever they may be. Freedom in this sense, if it is not identical with the absence of external impediments (to use the classic Hobbesian phrase), at least implies their absence. It is plain, however, that in an organized social setting, one cannot be free to do whatever one wishes. (Of course, I could be free to do whatever I wish, but then you wouldn't be free to do whatever you wish.) Organized society is by its very nature coercive and the potential for compulsion to act against one's wishes is ever present.

Anarchists might deny that this need be the case. But, at any rate, the simple answer will not do for societies as we know them. Social life, even without formal organization, has its inevitable coercive aspects. The demands of "public obligation" arise also within those publics-in-miniature such as the family, the school, and one's business. It is clear, however, that a society that has regard for individual freedom as an ideal or good will search for principles that limit the use of compulsion. The relationship of this problem to the debate over economic regulation that has raged throughout the nineteenth and twentieth centuries will not have escaped the reader.

---

[3] The subject of this chapter is dealt with from another point of view in Joel Feinberg's *Social Philosophy* (Englewood Cliffs, N.J.: Prentice-Hall, Inc., 1973), Chapters 2 and 3, in *Foundations of Philosophy Series*.

[4] Ibid., Chapter 1.

Now the problem of implementing the ideal of freedom in a social context is complicated by the fact that we are talking about the rights that a person should have: and these are not rights hanging in the air, but rather *protected rights*. A protected right implies the potential use of force or coercion against someone else. Consider one of the freedoms that I have—or think I have. I have the freedom—the protected right—to wear any tie that I own. This example only seems trivial. It may easily be extended to the question of the right of a high school student to wear his hair long, of the right of a bus driver or a policeman or an employee of a private firm to wear a beard, and of the right of a schoolteacher to wear a political button or armband. Such issues have been regarded as serious enough to be litigated (decisions of U.S. courts have gone both ways). It is in fact doubtful that an elementary school teacher has—or even ought to have—the protected right to wear a tie with the design of a nude woman or a racially derogatory remark on it. The seemingly trivial example of the tie symbolizes a class of complicated cases in which, if there is a protected right, a restraint on freedom is implied on others whose interests, desires, and tastes run in the opposite direction. One man's meat can be another man's poison. One's protected rights, therefore, are—to use Bentham's phrase—bought at the expense of somebody else's liberty.

**J. S. MILL
ON THE LIMITS
OF COERCION**

We shall return to the subject of protected rights toward the end of this chapter. Let us now take up some of the attempts at formulating principles for limiting the legal use of coercion. A natural starting place is the report of the Wolfenden Committee, issued in 1957, to which Devlin's lecture was a response.

This Committee was charged with the responsibility of inquiring into the English law on "homosexual offenses and prostitution" and making recommendations for its reform. In raising the question of limits the Committee stated:

Unless a deliberate attempt is to be made by society, acting through the agency of the law, to equate the sphere of crime with that of sin, there must remain a realm of private morality and immorality which is, in brief and crude terms, not the law's business.[5]

It is not the duty of the law to concern itself with immorality as such. . . . It should confine itself to those activities which offend against public order and decency or expose the ordinary citizen to what is offensive or injurious.[6]

[5] *The Wolfenden Report:* **Report of the Committee on Homosexual Offenses and Prostitution** (New York: Lancer Books, 1964), p. 52 (para. 61).

[6] Ibid., p. 169 (para. 257).

The Committee does not explain the terms "morality" and "immorality," but it is clear that they are understood to have a sexual connotation. In fact, the terms "ethics" and "morals" are no longer interchangeable in everyday speech. A governmental official arraigned on a "morals charge" will be accused of something quite different from one accused of an "ethics violation."

The expression "private morality," however, is meant to contrast with "public morality." These terms can be interpreted as marking (1) a distinction between what is done in private and what is done in public, (2) a distinction between an individual's personal ideals and the positive morality of a society, or (3) a distinction between acts that do not harm others and acts that do harm others. Clearly, these distinctions suggest a wider sphere of application than that to which the Wolfenden Committee was confined by its mandate. In addition to the so-called "victimless crimes" of consensual homosexuality and prostitution, we may consider not only such sex-related matters as bigamy, polygamy (an issue when Utah was admitted to the Union), incest, adultery, fornication, contraception, abortion, obscenity, and pornography but also the use of drugs and alcoholic beverages, gambling, euthanasia, and suicide.

The Wolfenden report, which is not a work of philosophy, quite naturally does not explain its limiting principle in detail. But it was quickly noticed that its spirit is akin to that of John Stuart Mill's essay *On Liberty*. In Mill the third of the above distinctions plays a central role. This is expressed in a paragraph that contains what Professor Hart has called Mill's "famous sentence":

The object of this Essay is to assert one very simple principle, as entitled to govern absolutely the dealings of society with the individual in the way of compulsion and control, whether the means used be physical force in the form of legal penalties, or the moral coercion of public opinion. That principle is, that the sole end for which mankind are warranted, individually or collectively, in interfering with the liberty of action of any of their number, is self-protection. That the only purpose for which power can be rightfully exercised over any member of a civilised community, against his will, is *to prevent harm to others*.[7] His own good, either physical or moral, is not a sufficient warrant.... The only part of the conduct of anyone, for which he is amenable to society, is that which concerns others. In the part which merely concerns himself, his independence is, of right absolute. Over himself, over his own body and mind, the individual is sovereign.[8]

This is the *locus classicus* of the position that there are spheres of con-

[7] This is the sentence to which Hart refers in his *Law, Liberty, and Morality* (Stanford: Stanford University Press, 1963), p. 4 [my italics].

[8] John Stuart Mill, *On Liberty*, first published in 1859 (Chicago: Gateway Edition, 1955), p. 13.

duct which are "not the law's business," although Mill does not confine himself to the law.

Mill recognizes certain exceptions to his "harm to others" principle: children, the feebleminded, and backward peoples. Here he allows paternalism; these persons may be restrained for their own good and not only when they are liable to cause harm to others. It is the case of the mature adult that "his own good is not a sufficient warrant" for compulsion. Mill's basic reason is that the individual is by far the best judge of his own interests. (Recent writers, such as Hart, are less sanguine than Mill on this point, and they are prepared to allow a greater degree of paternalism.) Mill also argues that when the law intervenes in the life of the individual in order to promote his good, it more often than not intervenes at the wrong point. It is difficult to see, however, that these contentions establish that such interventions are always illegitimate. They at most establish only a presumption to this effect. A good part of Mill's essay is given over to a defense of free speech. He presents the utilitarian argument that noninterference benefits society in the long run in the search for truth, and the same plea is put forward for "experiments in living" in the area of conduct that is not harmful to others. But, as the nineteenth-century writer James Fitzjames Stephen points out, the utilitarian argument cuts both ways: Why shouldn't the individual's freedom be limited if it promotes the general happiness and perhaps even his own happiness in the end? [9] Behind Mill's position is another important principle. It is that freedom is necessary for self-fulfillment. This is of real importance but it hardly establishes an "absolute" right to noninterference.

At any rate, though it is easy to sympathize with this "famous sentence," it is far from clear that it helps us very much. Mill's intention is to supply a single principle, and a very simple one at that, which enables us to isolate those spheres of conduct that legitimately are beyond the reach of the law and the "coercion" of public opinion. Does it do this? There are a number of issues here: Are there any kinds of actions of the sort envisioned by Mill—namely, actions that do not harm others? Is his principle all we need, or does it require supplementation of some kind? Is the principle really "simple"?

We might begin by noticing that the last statement quoted does not seem to follow from the previous ones. It is not true, even on Mill's own terms, that an individual is, without qualification, sovereign over his own body. Shall a pregnant woman be permitted to take thalidomide? Shall a person be permitted to conduct bizarre genetic experiments upon himself?

---

[9] *Liberty, Equality, Fraternity* (New York: Henry Holt, 1882). A good deal of this book is given over to a critique of Mill.

Such acts clearly may be matters that concern or harm others. Consider, also, a less exotic example. Most of the states, perhaps all, require a motorcyclist to wear a helmet. Arguing in a Millian fashion that the government lacks constitutional power to compel this, the Attorney General of New Mexico asserted that "it cannot be questioned that requiring a motorcycle rider to wear a helmet will render him less likely to be injured. However, if a motorcycle rider chooses to pursue his personal happiness by riding without a helmet it cannot be said that his choice will injure his fellow man." The latter statement, I think, is rather debatable. If the motorcyclist is injured, will not someone—a private party or the state—have to bear the burden of caring for the addlepated rider? In our welfare state anyone who engages in a high-risk activity is likely to become a public charge if injured, and there is therefore a social interest in reducing the risk. In such cases there is no reason to confine the state's interference merely to conduct that is, as Mill says, "calculated to produce evil in someone else." Now, Mill might well concede that these cases do come under the purview of the state. But my general point is that considerations similiar to the ones just mentioned can be brought against many of the cases which Mill and his spiritual descendents hold to be excluded from compulsion by his principle.

The difficulty with the assertion that an individual is sovereign over his mind and body is a special case of a more general difficulty. We simply cannot isolate, once and for all, spheres of conduct which inherently are not harmful to others or of no concern to others. (The terms "harmful to others" and "concerns others," while not literal equivalents, are used interchangeably by Mill.) This is to state in other words the notorious problem of distinguishing "self-regarding" from "other-regarding" actions, as Mill calls them. The issue is not merely whether there ever is conduct that is purely self-regarding (i.e., self-affecting), and thus beyond the reach of the law or "moral coercion." It may even be granted that instances of such conduct do occur. The question is, rather, whether the *kind* of conduct that is at issue is such that it is always self-regarding.[10] For the legislator, at least, must work by and large in terms of rules.

Mill is aware of this difficulty, and I think ends up by abandoning his simple principle. Thus, in the fourth chapter of his essay, Mill allows that many persons will not admit the distinction on which the principle

[10] Plainly, empirical data are necessary to answer such a question. It is not possible—without circularity—to define action types that never concern others. We may, however, now be in a fair position to say that certain kinds of actions are not likely to cause harm or are likely to cause only insignificant harm to others (assuming some definition of "harm"), and that such actions should not be subject to restraint. But this raises the issue of "inconvenience," which is discussed in the next few paragraphs.

rests, and he agrees "that the mischief which a person does to himself may seriously affect, both through their sympathies and their interests, those nearly connected with him and, in a minor degree, society at large." [11] Nevertheless, Mill insists that such injury would be merely contingent, the *inconvenience* of which society must bear for the sake of the greater good of human freedom, unless the individual violates a "specific duty to the public" or a "distinct and assignable obligation to any other person or persons." [12] With this insistence, however, Mill has cut the ground from under his principle.

First, it does no good to say that such conduct is taken out of the "self-regarding" class in case of these violations, unless we have already determined what the duties and obligations are. But this is precisely what Mill's principle, with its distinction between self-regarding and other-regarding conduct, is supposed to help us determine. Second, in his reference to "inconvenience," Mill is in effect saying that what is required is a *weighing* of the inconveniences against the good of human freedom. Mill is convinced, of course, that the latter will always outweigh the former. But is this necessarily so? Consider the case of unsightly advertising billboards placed on private property adjoining a public highway. Suppose, now, that the legislature is deciding whether to prohibit entirely or to restrict the size of such billboards. There is no question yet of a duty to the public. Nor is there injury to "assignable" individuals, whatever that may mean. Is it clear, though, that the "inconvenience" is one that society can afford to bear for the sake of the greater good of human freedom? Not so long ago, in the state of California particularly, there were large billboards proclaiming "Impeach Earl Warren" (the then Chief Justice of the U.S. Supreme Court). Suppose these billboards had contained a well-known four-letter Anglo-Saxon word in place of "Impeach." Would this have been an "inconvenience" that the public could have afforded to bear for the greater good of human freedom?

In implicitly acknowledging that there must be a weighing of the public's inconvenience against the good of human freedom, Mill really abandons his "simple principle." But even more crucial, however, is the question of what, after all, is meant by such terms as "inconvenience," "concern," "harm," "definite damage," etc. Without a specification of these meanings no weighing can take place. Behind the use of these terms is a series of moral and social assumptions that need to be made explicit.[13] When something is labeled an "inconvenience," for example, we mean that the interest that is affected is not of importance, or is of

11 Mill, *On Liberty*, p. 118.

12 Ibid., pp. 119 and 120.

13 See Ernest Nagel, "The Enforcement of Morals," in P. Kurtz, ed., *Moral Problems in Contemporary Society* (Englewood Cliffs, N.J.: Prentice-Hall, Inc., 1969), pp. 143 f.

lesser importance than some other interest. This needs to be spelled out in each case. Freedom, I believe, is an important human good. But it is not an unconditional good, and it can come into competition with other goods.

LEGISLATING
MORALITY

A recent writer, Professor Herbert Packer, in his important book *The Limits of the Criminal Sanction,* concedes that Mill's formula of "harm to others" solves very little. Nevertheless, Packer thinks it useful, because it makes sure that "a given form of conduct is not being subject to the criminal sanction purely or even primarily because it is thought to be immoral. It forces an inquiry into precisely what bad effects are feared if the conduct in question is not suppressed by the criminal law." [14] Notice here the distinction being suggested: immoral/bad effects. The criminal law can legitimately prohibit conduct of the latter sort, but not the former. What is the distinction between the two? In a subsequent discussion of criteria for the guidance of the legislator in the area of so-called "morals offenses," Packer includes among them that a certain form of conduct should not be made criminal if it can be shown that no secular harm results from the conduct. We have, then, a distinction between what is immoral, on the one hand, and what causes secular harm on the other.

Unfortunately, Professor Packer does not tell us what he means by the adjective "secular." A count shows at least fifty occurrences of the word in the book, but there is no attempt at any place to define it. Clearly, there are forms of conduct which everyone agrees are harmful: the use of violence in the commission of a crime, forcible rape, and homicide, for example. But then there is a whole range of activities that cannot be confidently classified unless we have some specified notion of secular harm.

Professor Louis Henkin presents a view similar to Packer's in an article entitled "Morals and the Constitution: the Sin of Obscenity." [15] Henkin maintains that there may be an argument on constitutional grounds against the intrusion of the law particularly into the suppression of obscenity. The suppression of obscenity, he says, is a deprivation of liberty that requires due process of law. One interpretation that he gives of this is that due process of law demands that legislation have a proper public purpose, and only a "rational, utilitarian social purpose" satisfies due process. The state may not legislate to preserve some traditional or

[14] *The Limits of the Criminal Sanction* (Stanford: Stanford University Press, 1968), p. 267.

[15] "Morals and the Constitution: the Sin of Obscenity," *Columbia Law Rev.,* 63 (1963), 391–414.

prevailing view of private morality. Henkin also goes on to argue that morals legislation is a relic of religious heritage, and the Constitution forbids such establishment of religion.

Here, then, we have a contrast very much like that of Professor Packer's: a contrast between private morals, which apparently are presumed to be matters of mere taste or to have a religious origin, and conduct that can be subjected to a rational, utilitarian examination. The difficulty with it is the same. It, too, requires further elaboration in terms of a system of moral and social assumptions in order to be applied to concrete legislative proposals. What is a rational, utilitarian social purpose? Is it the Benthamite notion of the maximization of pleasure, or is it something else? Perhaps it is a purpose on which there exists wide consensus in the society, but one cannot be sure.

Mill, as we noticed, admits various exceptions to his limiting principle. Many recent writers are prepared to go beyond Mill and permit legal coercion of mature adults for their "own good" in some cases. Hart defends this position, which he calls *legal paternalism*; he rejects *legal moralism*, the view that the law may prohibit conduct because it is immoral "as such." His argument for paternalism is that it is not always true that the individual is the best judge of his own interests. It is on this basis that he would defend a law restricting the sale of narcotics, and not on any alleged immorality of drug-taking. The requirement that a motorcyclist wear a helmet presumably would also be allowable on paternalistic grounds. Hart also says that laws "excluding the victim's consent as a defence to charges of murder and assault may perfectly well be explained as a piece of paternalism, designed to protect individuals against themselves." [16]

Having made this much of an inroad into Mill's principle of "harm to others," the question may be raised whether Hart shouldn't concede much more. Hart is unclear as to the scope of paternalism.[17] Moreover, it is not at all evident that the judgment that something is against someone's interest is not a moral judgment. Hart apparently agrees with the Wolfenden report that children should be protected from "corruption." But as Devlin argues in his discussion of the report, we have no reason to do this unless we believe that the activities involved are in some sense immoral. It has been suggested that paternalistic policies regarding a child are justified because when he becomes adult he will in retrospect acknowledge that they were in his interest. This presumes, I think, that the child will grow up to become a "normal" adult and make "normal" judgments. It is difficult, however, to disentangle judgments of normality

[16] Hart, *Law, Liberty, and Morality*, p. 31.

[17] Does paternalism mean, for example, that we should suppress conduct which in some respect is not in the actor's own interest but is socially valuable or morally heroic?

from moral judgments. In any event, paternalism does not leave us with a firm line for limiting the reach of the law.

Hart maintains that many existing legal prohibitions are not to be defended on the ground that they are attempts to enforce morality "as such," but on the ground that they protect the public from what is regarded as offensive. The crime of bigamy is used as an example. It would be illegitimate for the law to make bigamy a crime because it is inherently immoral or because it violates a religious injunction. Instead, the ground is that bigamy offends the sensibilities of people who believe in the sanctity of the marriage rite. Bigamy is a "nuisance." Now although the prohibition against bigamy could perhaps be defended in this way, it is doubtful that it is in fact the justification that generally would be offered in our society. As Professor Nagel points out, Hart begs the question if he assumes that the judgment that an act is a nuisance (or offensive) is always independent of a judgment on its morality.[18] I think that it would be said that bigamy is (and ought to be) a crime because it goes against an ideal of marriage and family life. The criminalization of bigamous marriage—i.e., making it a crime—is sometimes justified on the basis that such marriages upset property relationships and also might seriously affect our arrangements for the upbringing of children. This may be true. But these consequences are possible, in part, because of our view of family life. (I do not deny that this view is now under heavy assault, but this does not *ipso facto* imply that it is not the law's business to concern itself with the issue.)

PRIVACY

Where, then, does Hart draw the line? If he modifies Mill's formula of "harm to others," on what does Hart rest his position? If I understand him correctly, a basic—though not necessarily the only—criterion for determining the limits of the law is provided by the distinction between *acts done in public* and *acts done in private.* This emerges especially in his discussion of homosexual acts performed by consenting adults in private. It is, of course, well known that many laws in the sex-related area tend to be vague and leave much room for discretion on the part of law-enforcement agencies. There is a great deal of selective enforcement, and there are opportunities for blackmail, entrapment, etc. There is also hypocrisy: the nineteenth-century English law that criminalized male homosexuality left lesbianism untouched. (This should not be surprising; the law is a crazy-quilt.) Such facts, however, do not by themselves establish sharp limits to the law, and they are not Hart's main consideration.

Hart, I think, makes a *weighing,* a position to which Mill was also

18 Nagel, "The Enforcement of Morals," p. 155.

driven. The inconvenience—to use Mill's term—to the public that knows that in-private homosexual acts between consenting adults are performed and that feels distressed as a result carries little weight, and the social interest in prohibiting such conduct in private is surely small. It is easy to agree with Hart in this instance—*if* it is correct that all that is at stake is the distress felt by the public—and also with the general proposition that when an act is performed in private there is to that extent probably a lesser social interest in it in respect both of law and positive morality. Hart is obviously convinced that in the case of in-private homosexual acts the inconvenience is one that "society can afford to bear for the greater good of human freedom," as Mill puts it. Hart's own statement is very pointed: "No social order which accords to individual liberty any value could also accord the right to be protected from distress thus occasioned." [19]

Nevertheless, I think it clear that the mere fact that an act is done in private is *not* sufficient to take it out of the realm of public concern. Hart cannot possibly say that in-private sado-masochistic acts between consenting adults are beyond legal prohibition. Such acts come under paternalism, if anything does. Any paternalistic argument that would disallow the victim's consent as a defense against a charge of assault would also permit the criminalization of such acts. It would seem that the statement just quoted from Hart is partly a reflection of his views on sexuality. Sex urges are natural and powerful, and the suppression of them causes pain or great discomfort. This may be true, yet no society has existed without some regulation of sex. The question is where to draw the line, and this is a very difficult matter. Perhaps the public only feels a small degree of distress in the case of in-private homosexuality, but intense distress in the case of in-private desecration of a human corpse, for example.[20] Hart's weighing can take advantage of this difference. The quoted statement also seems to reflect the view that sexual morality is a matter of variable taste and convention. There is much truth to this. Nevertheless, ideals of proper conduct and living are not to be thrust completely aside. Certain sexual practices and "hard-core" pornography are humanly degrading, for they treat persons as things. There is, however, a very long step from morally condemning a practice to saying that it should be legally prohibited.

It is not clear how Hart would come out on other aspects of sexual morality. The proscription of homosexual acts between consenting adults in private, he finds unacceptable. But what about the legalization of

[19] Hart, *Law, Liberty, and Morality*, p. 47.

[20] See Louis B. Schwartz, "Moral Offenses and the Model Penal Code," in R. Wasserstrom, ed., *Morality and the Law* (Belmont, Calif.: Wadsworth Publishing Company, 1971), pp. 94 ff.

homosexual unions? This does not seem to be merely a matter of private activity, but bears upon rights and obligations vested in marriage and ideals of family life. One could not decide this issue solely on the basis of the distinction between in-private morality or immorality and public indecency. The decision to protect certain forms of conduct is not identical with the decision legally to tolerate such conduct. It is one thing, as Stephen says, "to tolerate vice so long as it is inoffensive, and quite another to give it a legal right, not only to exist but to assert itself in the face of the world as an 'experiment in living' as good as another, and entitled to the same protection from law." [21] Here it is especially important to keep in mind what was said earlier about protected rights. The question cannot be put simply in terms of what is not the law's business unless we mean to *withdraw* the law's protection. Moreover, in-private conduct has a way of "going public," as Stephen's remark suggests and as any big-city dweller can testify, and there is no reason to think that we should be less concerned here with the ends that the law ought to promote than we are in other branches of the law.

I would not like my last remark to be misunderstood. I am not arguing that activities of the sort we have been discussing ought necessarily to be criminalized. What I do maintain is that we have gone a long way from any simple limiting principle, and that no way has been provided to isolate spheres of conduct that are permanently beyond the reach of the law.

Although the location of an act may not seem a significant feature of it, great weight is accorded in-private activity by virtually every writer on the topic, including Lord Devlin, who stands in opposition to the rationale of the Wolfenden report. "As far as possible," says Devlin, "privacy should be respected." [22] Thus, in the formation of the law, "the claims of privacy" and "the public interest in the moral order" will have to be weighed in the balance especially when "all who are involved in the deed are consenting parties." [23] There are in fact significant points

---

21 Stephen, *Liberty, Equality, Fraternity,* p. 153.

22 Devlin, *The Enforcement of Morals,* p. 18. See also Stephen: "Legislation and public opinion ought in all cases whatever scrupulously to respect privacy" (*Liberty, Equality, Fraternity,* p. 160). But he gives this a rather interesting twist. Public indecency is an invasion of privacy. Privacy, he says, may be violated "by compelling or persuading a person to direct too much attention to his own feelings and to attach too much importance to their analysis.... Conduct which can be described as indecent is always in one way or another a violation of privacy." Stephen admits, however, that "there is a sphere, none the less real because it is impossible to define its limits, within which law and public opinion are intruders likely to do more harm than good" (p. 162).

23 Devlin, *The Enforcement of Morals,* p. 18. Devlin goes on to say that the "lesser acts" of homosexual indecency therefore should not be subject to criminal punishment. He has subsequently come to endorse the Wolfenden recommendation that the full offense should not be punishable.

of agreement between Devlin, Stephen, and Packer on factors that should be taken into account in the formation of the criminal law. For the law, as Stephen says, is a "rough engine" that needs to be controlled. Packer lists a number of these factors: for example, that suppressing the conduct in question is not inconsistent with the goals of punishment, that it can be dealt with through even-handed and nondiscriminatory enforcement, and that there are no reasonable alternatives to the criminal sanction for dealing with it.[24] Another important consideration is that criminalizing certain activities sometimes has the effect of giving criminals a monopoly over them.

Nevertheless, Devlin insists (and Stephen would agree) that "there is no theoretical limitation" to the law. If the preceding discussion is correct, this must be precisely the position of Mill, Packer, and Hart, also. I do not think that these writers are in the least entitled to dissent from Devlin's statement: "If the law on abortion causes unnecessary misery, let it be amended, not abolished on the ground that abortion is not the law's business. . . . The appointed lawmakers of society have a duty to balance conflicting values." [25]

DEVLIN ON LAW AND MORALS   We began this chapter with a reference to Devlin, but so far he has hardly been touched on. Let us now turn to him. Although, I believe, the negative proposition that he insists upon is correct, there are obscurities and difficulties in his position.

We may begin with an observation made by Devlin and most of the other participants in the controversy. In our pluralist society we believe that there should be freedom of religious belief, and a wide variety of religious practices is tolerated. Why, then, should this state of affairs not obtain with respect to morals as well? Devlin's answer is that a society is not just a people, but also a *community of ideas.* Common beliefs and attitudes about right and wrong and common standards of conduct are requisites of social life. In order to preserve itself, a society will, and also has the right to, inculcate these beliefs, attitudes, and standards in its members and demand compliance with them. A *public morality,* then, is essential to the existence of a society. Devlin draws an analogy that has become somewhat famous or infamous, depending on one's point of view: an analogy between immorality and treason. Both may impair the integrity of a society. And just as society has the right to use the law to prevent treason, so also it has the right to use the law to prevent im-

---

24 See Packer's useful discussion in *Limits of the Criminal Sanction,* Chap. 16.
25 Devlin, *The Enforcement of Morals,* p. 117.

morality. But here we must be cautious in interpreting Devlin. Even if society has a right to use the law to prevent breaches of public morality, it does not follow that society *ought* to use it. Devlin distinguishes the question of society's right to pass a moral judgment from the question of enforcing the judgment by law. There is no general answer to the second question; each case involves a balancing of values and practical considerations of the sort mentioned above. In the course of his exposition Devlin argues that the crime of bigamy, for example, and the rule that consent of the victim is not always a defense illustrate the fact that the law does enforce moral judgments. The same can be found also in the non-criminal branches of the law. We discussed this point in connection with Hart's paternalism.

Devlin's conception of a society as a community of ideas has been attacked as incompatible with the notion of a pluralist society. Professor Wollheim argues the liberal view that "the identity, and the continuity, of a society resides not in the common possession of a single morality but in the mutual toleration of different moralities." [26] I think this has considerable merit. Yet it can be argued with a great deal of plausibility that there are limits to toleration even in a pluralist society. No society can be completely pluralist in the stated sense, especially if we keep in mind what is involved in according protected rights. Moreover, it may well be the case that the viability of a pluralist society does presuppose some common agreement among different moralities, a common core. It has been suggested, on the other hand, that the crucial feature of a pluralist society is common agreement on procedures and institutions, not on moral opinions and values. This also has merit, but I think it can be overstressed. A pluralist society is not a debating club without any interest or expectations about what will emerge from its accepted process. Devlin is not opposed to toleration. But he is not entirely clear on how much he would allow.

Devlin maintains that the right of a society to have a public morality and to use the law to enforce it derives from its right to preserve itself. This, says Hart, requires the implausible assumption that a society is somehow identical with its morality, for only then can a breach of the morality be destructive of it. It also follows that the morality of a society could not change without the society's having been by definition destroyed and replaced by a new one. But this seems ludicrous. Devlin, however, has replied that he does not deny that the morality of a society may change. Moreover, he asserts that if the law is used to enforce morality, it should change (but slowly) in response to a change in morality. His position is that deviation from the shared morality *may*

26 Richard Wollheim, "Crime, Sin and Mr. Justice Devlin," *Encounter* (November 1959), p. 38.

threaten its existence, and therefore there is no theoretical limit to the law. We suppress treasonous activities because they may threaten society's existence, not because any given subversive act *will* destroy it. The law can be used to enforce morality as something that is essential to a society.

We can see from his examples what it is that Devlin has in mind to some extent. If someone gets drunk every night in the privacy of his home, who is the worse for it? Drunkenness, to use Mill's language, is just someone's experiment in living. "But suppose," asks Devlin, "a quarter or a half of the population got drunk every night, what sort of society would it be? You cannot set a theoretical limit to the number of people who can get drunk before society is entitled to legislate against drunkenness." [27] Similarly for homosexuality and fornication. He concedes, however, that a society may be prepared to tolerate both as long as they are confined.

All this seems reasonable to me, but the difficulty is that it is still not at all clear that deviation from public morality, even when widespread, threatens society's *existence,* or even what this means. What are the spheres of morality that are in fact essential to a society? Is it essential to our society that the distribution of pornographic literature be prohibited? Is it essential that gambling be prohibited? There seems to be an ambiguity in Devlin's position. On the one hand, he apparently holds that indulgence in "vice" does weaken a person or a society. A society may "disintegrate" from within as well as be destroyed by external attack. On the other hand, Devlin sometimes seems to hold that the crucial thing is merely whether a society *believes* that its existence is threatened by certain activities.

How is the public morality ascertained? Devlin refers us to a figure familiar to the English lawyer: the man in the Clapham omnibus, the right-minded man, the reasonable man. What counts is the cross-section of society represented by the twelve men in the jury box. The public morality is determined by the moral judgments of the right-minded man, and these judgments are conceded to be largely matters of feeling. Devlin's opponents seize on this. Hart argues that it is precisely when public feeling is high that thought is needed on the part of the legislator, who should be guided by rational rather than emotional considerations. This criticism, I think, is a bit off the mark. Devlin does use such language as "a real feeling of reprobation," "disgust," and "abhorrence." But it is used in connection with determining the limits of toleration, for he maintains that nothing should be punished unless it lies beyond these limits. Moreover, Devlin requires that the moral judgment should be deliberate. He tells us that we should look at homosexuality calmly and dispassionately

---

[27] Devlin, *The Enforcement of Morals,* p. 14. Stephen's remark, quoted in the text on p. 63, is also appropriate here.

and ask ourselves whether we regard it as a vice so "abominable" that its mere presence is an offense. Most Americans, I believe, are revolted by the thought of eating cockroaches, but on reflection they would not think of making it a crime. Still, there is something to Hart's objection, for Devlin also maintains that while the educated person (Hart's "rationalist" moralist) can try to influence public opinion, the legislator has a duty to follow the public morality whatever its worth. This is democracy with a vengeance. It may even be viewed as one of the "paradoxes of democracy," for shouldn't the legislator be responsive to the popular will even if it means resticting someone's freedom? A main problem, however, is that Devlin tends to assume a greater convergence of moral opinion than probably exists. It is also not clear how all this harmonizes with Devlin's statement that lawmakers have a duty to balance conflicting values. And balancing is essential if society is going to accord protected rights.

Despite these difficulties, Devlin's main point stands: there are no theoretical limitations to the law. I do not think this is in any way negated by Hart's "critical principle, central to morality, that human misery and the restriction of freedom are evils." [28] To this I would add that restraint is an evil because freedom is a good. But it is not the only good, and freedom sometimes has to be restricted in order to achieve other goods. Mill quite rightly stresses the importance of freedom. There is reason to believe that without it there is no social progress and no moral development, just as a child without freedom will never become an adult in the best sense. (But discipline is also necessary.) If we give a high priority to freedom it is because of the view we have of the good life.

The limits of the law will have to be settled on an issue-by-issue basis. Very often we will disagree on its reach because we disagree over the possible consequences of a policy. Solidly grounded social knowledge is therefore indispensable. Some disagreements will result from disagreements on quasi-empirical issues. Abortion is a case in point. Is abortion the killing of a human being? The answer surely bears on the question of whether or not a foetus deserves the protection of law. What, furthermore, does the value that we put on life commit us to in respect of a foetus? And what are the moral implications of any answer we give?

The question of *values* cannot be avoided. This is so even if we proceed on an issue-by-issue basis, for we need their guidance in order to assess consequences and facts and in order to weigh competing interests. We cannot specify the limits of the law without indicating the values that the legal system should promote. We need at least a provisional conception of the good life, in which freedom is an ingredient. This conception should be open to criticism and to revision and extension. Obviously, in

28 Hart, *Law, Liberty, and Morality*, p. 82.

a pluralist society there will be many views on this, and toleration is indispensable. This does not mean that one must refrain from promoting one's view, although the instrumentality of law should be used cautiously and thoughtfully.

The view of the good life that is relevant here is not that of the isolated and self-sufficient individual, but of the individual in society. We therefore also need a conception of the good society. I am far from being able to say what such a society is. But I have no doubt that a *free* society is one that takes the risk of allowing the individual to do what might be bad, harmful, or foolish. But the issue cannot be left in this condition. For this allowance cannot be unlimited. A morality of laissez faire produces a society without protected rights. Claims to freedoms have to be balanced. A free society, then, will have to concern itself with the question of what a good society is and what ingredients of freedom it embodies. The question is inescapable though its answer eludes us.

CHAPTER FOUR

Punishment: The Deterrence Theory

Legal theories which affirm a necessary connection between laws and sanctions are the products of philosophical sophistication. For the ordinary citizen, some such connection is likely to appear as sheer common sense. He thinks of the law largely in terms of its criminal branch, in which law and law enforcement seem inextricably bound together. The symbol of the law is not so much the lawmaker as the police officer, whose job is that of preventing crime, detecting its occurrence, and apprehending the malefactor. And the process of law enforcement does not stop here. Its culmination is the punishment of the criminal after the elaborate ritual of trial and conviction.

Each stage in this process raises questions of an ethical or moral sort, but none has been so controversial as punishment. By what right do we punish? Is punishment ever justified at all? What is a just punishment? Is capital punishment, for example, just or humane? Who should be held responsible for his actions and, hence, punishable? When is it appropriate to excuse someone from punishment? These questions have called forth diverse answers and have even generated skepticism about the whole business of punishment. At one extreme, some psychiatrists and social scientists have maintained that punishment is itself a "crime" or almost never justifiable, and they have called for its replacement by treatment and cure. Legal philosophers, on the other hand, have generally held that punishment can be justified, but they have disagreed over its grounds. We should not, however, view the issue as a controversy between philosophy and psychiatry or social science. The basic philosophical task is not that of justifying or rejecting any particular system of punishment, but rather elaborating the considerations that are relevant to arriving at reasoned judgments regarding punishment and responsibility.

THE PROBLEM OF JUSTIFICATION

What is punishment and why does it call for justification? It is commonly pointed out that the term "punishment" is sometimes used metaphorically. If I stub my toe in the dark or catch a cold after having gone out in bad weather, I might say that I was punished for my carelessness, but this would be a metaphorical use of the term. We shall see later that some philosophers have maintained that the proper definition of "punishment" is a matter of importance. At present it is enough for us to recognize that we can identify *clear cases* of punishment, and these are especially to be found in the law when an authority punishes someone for his having committed an offense. In these cases pain or some loss (of life, freedom, rights, or property) is deliberately imposed on the individual. Furthermore, this is done without his consent, if not against his will. Now it is prima facie morally wrong deliberately to inflict pain or loss on a person without his consent. Hence the problem of justification: can such deliberate imposition of pain or loss be justified?

This kind of problem also arises in other contexts. Many people in our society are confined, in a sense imprisoned, without their consent. Among them are persons who have communicable diseases, are mentally ill, or are unable to care for themselves. We do not usually regard the deprivations imposed in these situations as instances of punishment, but a similar, and not always easier, problem of justification also arises for them. Of course, there are important differences between them and punishment. As Bishop Butler points out, our attitude toward the imprisoned criminal is quite different from our attitude toward someone who is quarantined because of measles or smallpox.[1] Distinctively associated with the notion of punishment are such ideas as wrongdoing, guilt, blame, desert, and condemnation. As we discuss various theories of punishment, we shall want to see what role these ideas play in them. It should be equally clear, on the other side, that as long as deliberate

[1] Joseph Butler, "A Dissertation upon the Nature of Virtue," in his *The Analogy of Religion* (London, 1736).

deprivation without consent is involved, the issue of justification cannot be avoided merely by adopting a more "medical" or "therapeutic" approach to the offender and seemingly throwing out punishment and the ideas that are associated with it.

The problem of the justification of punishment, as Hart has pointed out, has three principal facets: (1) Why should we punish at all; what is the justifying purpose of punishment? (2) Whom are we justified in punishing? (3) How and how much may we justifiably punish? [2] It is debatable whether these questions can be treated in complete isolation from one another. Still, the traditional theories of punishment may differ as to their relevance in answering these questions. One theory may be more appropriate, for instance, to "Why punish at all?" than to "Whom shall we punish?"

It is important to see that the problem of the justification of punishment should not be confused with the question of prison reform. The source of this confusion may be question 3. Prison reform is mainly concerned with what to do with the offender *while* he is being punished. Improvement in facilities, counseling, job training, etc. can be equally welcomed by proponents of opposed philosophical theories of punishment. Inhumane or brutal treatment—which, sad to say, is too much a part of prison life—can in general be "justified" only by *misapplying* these theories. Such treatment is no more an aspect of the punishment that philosophers have usually been concerned to justify than visits by the local orchestra or prison chaplain. These visitations, like bad treatment, are part of what happens to the inmate while he is being punished, and are not necessarily part of his punishment as such.

Before we turn to these theories there is one more point for us to consider. It is related to the definition of "punishment." Our focus of interest is, of course, legal punishment, and legal punishment typically presupposes three things: (1) a set of laws, (2) a procedure for determining who shall be punished as a way of enforcing the laws, and (3) an authoritative social mechanism for imposing the punishment. When these conditions exist in a society, the society may be said to have an *institution of legal punishment.* Now it is true, as I have already suggested, that many recent writers define this institution in stricter terms. At the moment, however, there is an advantage to our looser definition; namely, that it is neutral as between different justifications of punishment. The same can be said about the term "law enforcement" as used here. No theory is committed to denying that in punishing, the law is typically being enforced. We should not, at this stage, build into the

[2] See Hart's important article, "Prolegomenon to the Principles of Punishment," in H. L. A. Hart, *Punishment and Responsibility* (Oxford: Clarendon Press, 1968), pp. 1–27.

definition of the institution the moral elements that many writers hold to be required by any sound theory of punishment. With this background we can now turn to the question of whether, and on what basis and under which conditions, legal punishment is justified.

There are two main rival kinds of theories of punishment, the *deterrent* and the *retributive*. A third kind of theory, the *reformative*, which was first suggested by Plato, is also found, often as an appendage to the others. Now it is tempting to resolve this rivalry as common sense does, by saying that legal punishment should encompass all three. It should deter people from committing crimes, exact retribution from the criminal, and also reform him. It is questionable whether such a resolution is consistently possible. Each theory seems entangled in difficulties. In the name of deterrence, the first theory apparently permits the punishment of the innocent and punishment out of proportion to the gravity of the offense. Retribution seems to presuppose an assessment of moral wickedness that is beyond the competence of the law to make and hence degenerates into mere revenge. Finally, it is doubtful that punishment as such can reform; it seems only to harden the criminal as an enemy of society. We shall begin our examination with the deterrence theory.[3]

THE DETERRENCE THEORY

The idea that punishment serves as a deterrent to crime or other wrongdoing is, of course, very ancient (see e.g., Deut. 21:21), but probably the oldest statement of the deterrence theory is given in Plato's *Laws* (xi, 934):

> Punishment is not retribution for the past, for what has been done cannot be undone; it is imposed for the sake of the future and to secure that both the person punished and those who see him punished may either learn to detest the crime utterly or at any rate to abate much of their old behavior.

Taking this as an epitome of the justification of legal punishment in terms of deterrence, we see that the theory is *teleological* in character. Punishment is not a good in itself; it is justified by reference to the good consequence (reduction of crime) it presumably brings about. This constitutes the justifying aim or end, and punishment is the means. The deterrence theory is *forward-looking*, because this consequence lies in the future of the time at which a punishment is imposed. Retributivism is usually contrasted with this theory on precisely these points: it affirms the rightfulness, independently of any good consequences that might result, of punishing an offender—but only if he is morally accountable—

---

[3] Because the reformative theory is often incorporated into the other theories and into the view that rejects punishment, we shall not give it separate consideration.

because he (past fact) committed a crime. Some recent writers have proposed a kind of amalgamation of both theories. They maintain that the aim of deterrence justifies having the *institution* of legal punishment while backward-looking considerations justify punishing *given individuals* (offenders). The deterrence theory answers to "Why punish at all?" and something like retributivism answers to "Whom shall we punish?" We shall come back to this later.

Justification of punishment in terms of deterrence clearly rests upon an empirical premise; namely, that punishment in fact deters people from committing crimes. A standard objection against the deterrence theory is that punishment in fact does *not* deter, as evidenced by the extraordinary rate of recidivism, and also by the fact that the criminal now standing before the judge and awaiting his sentence was obviously not deterred by the prospect. The mere occurrence of crime, it is claimed, shows the impotence of punishment. It would be better to try to reduce crime by eliminating its causes.

To deal with this objection we need to introduce two distinctions: first, a distinction between the *threat* of punishment and its actual *imposition*. The criminal law exists basically to tell people that there are certain acts, which are regarded as socially harmful, which society does not want done, and it re-enforces this by threatening punishment. This point is written into the stricter definitions of the institution of legal punishment. Legal punishment typically presupposes a system of laws, and these are laws that specify offenses and threaten punishments for their commission.

Now there seem to be good grounds for believing that many people *are* deterred from committing some acts by the threat of punishment. Aside from self-observation, this is supported by crime increase during police strikes and by obedience to regulations promulgated by an occupying power in wartime. It is of course true that the offender who is now being punished was not deterred by that prospect from committing his act, but the threat may well have deterred him from committing more acts of the same kind. (The fact that I have been fined for parking violations does not show that I was never deterred from committing them.) Everyone can applaud the idea of dealing with crime by eliminating its causes, but it is most implausible to propose doing away with penal laws, laws that threaten punishment for specified offenses.

The second distinction is between *particular* and *general* deterrence. Whether or not an offender's actual punishment will deter *him* from committing future crimes of the same kind—this is what is meant by "particular deterrence"—depends partly on the punishment he gets. If he is executed, the punishment will be completely effective. If he is imprisoned, he is deterred, prevented, during his incarceration, at least.

It is also conceivable, though unlikely, that the punishment will bring about a change of heart and reform him. The big question is whether imprisonment will strike enough terror in his heart so as to discourage him from committing crimes after his release. The high recidivism rate is evidence to the contrary. But it is not conclusive, in the present state of our knowledge.

In any case the main interest of the deterrent theorist is general deterrence—that is, that punishing the offender deters *others* from committing acts of the same kind, thus reducing crime. General deterrence, as Bentham says, is the "chief end" and "real justification" of legal punishment. Against this, Mabbott, a retributivist, objects that it is still not the actual punishment that deters these others but rather the threat of it; it is therefore wrong to justify *inflicting* the punishment by reference to general deterrence. This seems incorrect, for carrying out the threat when it falls due is what gives it teeth. A second and related retributivist objection is put by Kant. General deterrence involves *using* the criminal as an instrument. But no one should be used as a mere means, even for the good of society. What right, we may ask, do we have to use someone in this way? The deterrent theorist's reply to this is that it is unfortunate that we have to punish at all, and in any case we may justifiably use someone as a means to promote a greater good. As we shall see shortly, however, the retributivist's objection cuts deeper than this.

But does general deterrence work? Granted that the offender who is incarcerated or executed is prevented from committing crimes, does this deter others? Studies of capital punishment, for example, have at least cast doubt on its effectiveness as a deterrent to murder. Similarly, repeaters and growing crime rates cast general doubt on the punitive approach to the problem of crime; perhaps it would be better to deal with the causes of crime.

This attack on the empirical basis of the deterrence theory has already been partially answered. The evidence against general deterrence is far from conclusive. Moreover, we know precious little about the causes of crime (although there is a high correlation between certain crimes and economic class) and even less about how to eliminate them. The problem is at any rate formidable, and until the millennium comes it seems that society cannot afford to give up some form of punishment.[4] In any case, the counterevidence need not embarrass the deterrence theorist. For his position can be construed as saying that deterrence is ethically *relevant* to whether we ought to punish and, furthermore, it is the *only* ethically relevant consideration. To understand this, we need to go more deeply into the philosophical underpinnings of the theory in its classical form.

[4] On these points, see the still useful article by Morris R. Cohen, "Moral Aspects of the Criminal Law," in his *Reason and Law* (New York: Collier Books, 1961), pp. 25–72.

THE UTILITARIAN THEORY   The most ardent supporters of the deterrence justification have been the hedonistic utilitarians.

Hedonistic utilitarianism is an ethical doctrine which holds that (only) pleasure is intrinsically good and (only) pain is intrinsically bad. The rightness of a particular act or—in some versions —of a type of act depends on its tendency to maintain or increase the balance of pleasure over pain in the society. The only justifiable reason for inflicting pain is that otherwise there would be more pain or less pleasure. Punishment, though itself unpleasant and therefore intrinsically bad, can be justified insofar as it maintains or increases the balance of pleasure over pain by discouraging harmful (pain-producing) behavior. This is the classical *utilitarian-deterrence* theory. In a nutshell, individuals are punished for the good (overall happiness) of society.[5]

The objections to this theory are obvious. First of all, if the reason, and only reason, for punishing is the good of society—if, as Kant would say, we are justified in using someone as a means to this end—why confine punishment to criminals? Why not punish the innocent? After all, what counts in deterring others from committing crimes is not that the punished person *has* committed an offense but rather the general *belief* that he has. The utilitarian-deterrence theory seems to allow "framing" innocent persons in the name of deterrence. Moreover, although it may be conceded that the criminal law is initially designed to deter the potential offender by threatening him with punishment, why should its imposition be confined to actual offenders if all we are interested in is deterrence? Most parents would be just as deterred from committing crimes if they knew that the threatened consequences would be imposed on their children instead of themselves. On the utilitarian-deterrence view there seems to be nothing wrong with visiting the sins of wicked fathers on innocent sons.

The second kind of objection bears on the issue of how much we should punish. The utilitarian-deterrence theory seems to permit unjust punishments—e.g., severe penalties for minor offenses. It may be possible to deter parking violations by cutting off an arm or by a long prison sentence, but this would be *unjust to the offender*. Punishment should "fit" the crime and be proportionate to the blameworthiness of the offender. (It is not clear that these are the same thing.) If the proper end of punishment, as the eighteenth-century utilitarian William Paley

---

[5] The clear cases of punishment, as we have seen, can involve loss of rights, freedom, or property. According to the above view, these are also experienced as painful. But I doubt that this is necessarily the case, if "pain" is understood literally. Secondly, one may experience pleasure in meting out punishment. Hedonistic utilitarians (e.g., Bentham) deny that this sort of pleasure should be credited toward the overall happiness. I do not find the arguments on this score consistent, but a general discussion of the doctrine is out of place here.

says, is "the prevention of crimes," we are led to the conclusion that it does not matter whether punishment is "proportionable to the guilt of the criminal or not." [6] But this conclusion is repugnant to the sense of justice.

These objections attack the classical utilitarian-deterrence theory at its very heart. At stake is the moral basis of punishment as an institution and in its particular applications. No justification is morally acceptable if it "justifies" injustice, and this is what the theory apparently does. It seems to permit punishing the innocent and punishing the criminal out of proportion to the gravity of his offense. The source of the difficulty is clear: the theory contains no essential reference to such retributivist concepts as guilt, moral accountability, desert, and blameworthiness, which are ingredients of the common concept of punitive justice. Any such reference, moreover, seems barred, for it introduces the sort of nonteleological and non-forward-looking ethical considerations that have no place in hedonistic utilitariansim.

HARSH PUNISHMENTS

We shall shortly examine "revisionist" utilitarian replies to our objections. It will be instructive first to consider Jeremy Bentham's treatment of the second objection. Bentham, a hedonistic utilitarian, is one of the most profound and thoroughgoing thinkers on the criminal law. What sense, after all, can be given to the idea of fitting the punishment to the crime? Bentham deals with this in detail. His underlying idea is that the prevention of mischief should be pursued only when it is *worthwhile* to do so, as determined by hedonistic utilitarian considerations. This, and not any appeal to justice or natural rights, fixes the limits of law and legal punishment.[7]

Bentham sets out various kinds of cases for which punishment is not worthwhile. The main one for our purposes is composed of cases in which punishment is "unprofitable"; i.e., the sum of the harm it produces is greater than the sum of the mischief it seeks to prevent. A cost-benefit analysis is needed in order to determine which acts should be criminalized and what the punishment for them should be. All this obviously presupposes some way of calculating and comparing the amounts of pain (and other losses calculable in terms of pain and lost opportunities for pleasure) in a proposed offense and in a proposed punishment. Bentham's advance over earlier utilitarians is his working

---

[6] Cited from Paley's *Principles of Moral and Political Philosophy* in Edmund L. Pincoffs, *The Rationale of Legal Punishment* (New York: Humanities Press, 1966), p. 18.

[7] Jeremy Bentham, *An Introduction to the Principles of Morals and Legislation,* first published in 1789 (New York: Hafner Publishing Company, 1961), Chaps. 13–15.

out a "calculus" for these purposes. He also presents a detailed analysis of types of offense.

In deciding whether a certain harm (e.g., arson, rape, burglary, overtime parking, etc.) ought to be prevented, the legislature must also determine the "lot" of *threatened* punishment that would have to be annexed to it. Bentham lays down a number of rules for determining such amounts. The two most important rules state, in effect, that the amount should be (1) enough to counterbalance the temptation to commit the given offense and (2) no more than is enough. Plainly, if the fine for overtime parking on the street is one dollar and it costs two dollars to park in a garage, the temptation to commit the offense will not be counterbalanced by the prospect of punishment. On the other hand, a ten-dollar fine may be more than is necessary. Bentham assumes not only that the legislature can make such utilitarian calculations but also that the average citizen can and will too. "All men calculate." This model of man as a rational calculator and actor, which is assumed by the deterrence theory, has been called into question in recent years, especially since the rise of depth psychology.

On Benthamite principles, then, we should punish no more and no less than is necessary to prevent an offense (assuming the offense in question to be one that may profitably be prevented). This, rather than any retributivist "moral fit" to the gravity of the crime or blameworthiness, is Bentham's solution to the problem of proportioning punishments to offenses. Punishing more than is necessary is cruelty to the criminal; punishing less than is necessary is cruelty to the unprotected public, and also a waste of the inflicted pain. Bentham holds steadfastly to the forward-looking goal of preventing mischief at the "cheapest rate" possible.[8]

Although it is of the first importance to take social costs, including costs to offenders, into account in formulating and enforcing the criminal law, Bentham's position is beset with difficulties. Even assuming that we can make the required calculations, his approach is unworkable. *Prevention* of mischief, literally understood, is not a feasible goal unless we are prepared to use draconian and unjust punishments. The punishment necessary—no more, no less—to prevent crime will usually have to be very severe, and even then crime will not be completely prevented. All we can reasonably hope to do is *reduce* the incidence of mischief. We in fact expect crime to occur, and by threatening the potential offender we hope to keep crime within limits, however unpalatable this may seem. In deciding whether it is worthwhile to reduce a given harm to a certain level, we do have to consider the amount of threatened punishment that

---

[8] Bentham's rules lead to conclusions that are contrary to some current penal practices— e.g., remission of sentence (time off) for good behavior in jail.

would be necessary. But I see no reason why, in weighing the matter, the pain that would have to be inflicted on wrongdoers should be given a consideration equal to that of the pain that would otherwise be suffered by their potential victims.

It seems to me morally more compelling that the innocent public should be protected from cruelty than the wrongdoer. This does not necessarily mean that offenders deserve to be punished, as the retributivist would have it, but that innocent potential victims are entitled to protection. This is at least part of the basis of *the right to punish,* even at the price, sometimes, of inflicting a greater total amount of pain in punishment than the total amount of harm eliminated. If a society could prevent a third murder by executing the perpetrators of the first two (leaving aside the question of the humaneness of capital punishment), it would appear justified in doing so although it means killing two people to save one. (Or ought we to conclude, because there would now be four dead, that the murderers should be let off because then there would only be three dead, namely, the innocent victims?) None of this implies, of course, the permissibility of harsh penalties for trivial offenses.

A very basic difficulty in Bentham's approach is that it requires a mass of impossible calculations and projections. Moreover, we do not seem able to make the necessary kinds of comparisons: quantitative comparisons between A's pleasure and pain as against B's pleasure and pain, and even between A's pleasure and A's pain. It is still to Bentham's credit that he worked out a "calculus." Many recent writers speak of equalizing benefit and distress in fixing punishments, but they do not say how this is to be determined except by intuition or guesswork.

Most contemporary utilitarians do not accept Bentham's calculative hedonism, but still defend a utilitarian-deterrence position. Professor Benn, who is in this modern movement, argues that utilitarianism can be formulated in a way that does not justify harsh punishments for minor offenses. He maintains that the proposition "trivial crimes do not deserve severe penalties" is a tautology, because the "seriousness" and "triviality" of offenses are to be defined relative to the suffering we are willing to inflict in order to deter them. In selecting the punishment for a given type of crime we are expressing a *preference* for (not a quasi-quantitative comparison of) one state of affairs to another; i.e., that the marginal increment of mischief inflicted on offenders is preferable to the mischief that would otherwise be suffered by the community. One parking offense more or less is not of great moment, but one murder more or less is, and we are prepared to punish more severely in the latter cases than in the former.[9]

[9] S. I. Benn, "An Approach to the Problems of Punishment," *Philosophy,* 33 (1958), 325–41.

This solution does not appear adequate, although Benn's position is an advance over Bentham's. It is certainly true in one sense that a serious offense is one for which we are prepared to impose a relatively heavy punishment. In this sense sheep-stealing *was* at one time as serious an offense as murder in England, because both were punished by hanging. But as H. J. McCloskey points out, this does not mean that any crime punished by hanging is a grave crime in the morally significant sense of the term.[10] Murder is not a morally graver crime than overtime parking because we are prepared to punish murder more severely. On the contrary, we are prepared to punish murder more severely because we regard it a morally graver offense. Our readiness to punish in a certain amount is partly conditioned by the relative importance of the *interest* or *value* (e.g., life, social convenience) that is thereby protected or affirmed. There is some basis, therefore, for Mabbott's view that we reserve our heaviest penalties for what are socially the most serious wrongs regardless of whether these penalties are exactly what deterrence would require.[11] If this is correct, the proposition "trivial offenses do not deserve severe penalties" is not a tautology.

Put in other words, even if we adopt a deterrence theory of the *purpose* of punishment (especially for having such an institution), we should not completely abandon the idea of a "moral fit" between the *amount* of punishment and crime. I am not convinced that Benn really abandons this idea, for he speaks of offenses for which we feel "justified" in imposing heavier penalties, and this is not determined solely by reference to the deterrent effects of a punishment or by simple utilitarian considerations. Benn admits that his position does not answer the question of whether few offenders should be given severe penalties or many offenders should be given light penalties. If this is a matter of preference, it surely is one which to some extent depends upon the relative importance of the affected interest and the relative moral gravity of the offense. The fact that people disagree on their estimates of these matters is no more an objection against this view than disagreement over preferences is an objection against Benn's variety of utilitarianism. (In the last analysis it is not entirely clear how thoroughgoing Benn's utilitarianism is, once he departs from Bentham's calculative hedonism.)

**PUNISHING
THE INNOCENT** We have thus far been considering how the utilitarian-deterrence theorist may deal with the objection that his position permits harsh punishments for minor offenses. Our second, and perhaps more serious, objection

[10] "A Non-Utilitarian Approach to Punishment," *Inquiry,* 8 (1965), 249–63.

[11] J. D. Mabbott, "Punishment," *Mind,* 49 (1939), 152–67.

was that the theory also justifies the punishment of the innocent. There seems to be nothing explicit in Bentham that answers this objection, although he clearly has in view only the punishment of actual offenders. Recent exponents of the theory do address the problem frontally.

It is occasionally argued that the punishment of the innocent is in fact sometimes justifiable—e.g., when a catastrophe can be averted by framing an innocent man. Abstractly speaking, this is well taken, but it is also fraught with danger. In the *Dreyfus* case the accused was the victim of an anti-Semitic plot, and many outraged persons sought to vindicate him. Others conceded the injustice to Captain Dreyfus but nevertheless claimed that the honor of the French general staff and, ultimately, the security of the country were at stake. It is easy to see how this argument can become a slippery slope that will tolerate monstrous injustice. How momentous must some "evil" be in order to allow the punishment of the innocent? In any event, the argument plainly involves the sacrifice of an important principle of justice. Even if we are justified in sometimes punishing the innocent, we do so at the price of giving up a principle that should ordinarily prevail and that appears to have value independent of utilitarian-deterrent considerations.

Another reply to the objection has, with some minor variations, been put forward by Quinton, Flew, and Benn.[12] Hart calls it the "definitional stop." [13] This reply maintains that retributivism is correct insofar as it holds that only the guilty should be punished: guilt *is* a necessary condition of punishment, but this is merely a "logical" point about the meaning of the word "punishment." The deterrence theory is mainly concerned to justify, on utilitarian grounds, the imposition of rules of conduct that threaten unpleasantness to those who violate them. Someone cannot be said to be guilty unless his action falls under such a rule, and he cannot be said to be punished unless the unpleasantness is a consequence of having violated the rule. The deterrence theory is a justification of *punishment* and not of any and every infliction of unpleasantness. It is logically impossible to punish the innocent, so the deterrence theory could never justify it.

This reply is unsatisfactory. If the reason we are justified in having (and, of course, also applying) rules that threaten punishment is the *general* deterrence of crime, the question still remains whether this does not also justify framing and then inflicting unpleasantness on an innocent person. (It might even be "cheaper.") We may refuse to call this

---

[12] A. M. Quinton, "On Punishment," *Analysis,* 14 (1954), 133–42; A. Flew, "The Justification of Punishment," *Philosophy,* 29 (1954), 291–307; Benn, "An Approach to the Problems of Punishment," 325–41.

[13] Hart, "Prolegomenon to the Principles of Punishment," *Punishment and Responsibility,* p. 6.

"punishment," if we wish. Instead, let us call it "victimization," as Honderich suggests,[14] and it appears that the utilitarian-deterrence theory permits victimizing an innocent person whom the public believes to be guilty. And even if this were justifiable in extreme cases, it would nevertheless be *unjust* to the one who is victimized.

A second difficulty is that the concepts of guilt and punishment have not been so restricted as Quinton, Flew, and Benn seem to suggest. Guilt has been *imputed* to individuals because of their membership in a certain group (collective guilt), and what was meted out to them was certainly regarded as punishment. But this is precisely what many retributivists object to. They insist that only *personal* guilt can be a justifiable condition of inflicting punishment. If the concept of guilt is broad enough to allow for collective guilt, the claim that punishment should require personal guilt is not just a logical point about the meaning of words. (It should be noted that the law does in fact mete out punishment "vicariously"—e.g., when it penalizes the tavern owner whose employee sells liquor to an underage person without the owner's knowledge.)

The "definitional stop" (punishment of the innocent is not really punishment), therefore, is no answer to our objection. As Professor Hart points out, it clouds the important issue of the moral status of the preference for a system of social control under which painful measures are meted out only on actual offenders *versus* systems of "social hygiene" which dispense with the notion of guilt and which are favored by the modern critics of punishment.

The last reply we shall consider is one that is developed in detail by John Rawls and also suggested by Quinton, Flew, and Benn. Our objection, it will be recalled, says that the utilitarian-deterrence theory would justify punishing an innocent person if it *paid* to do so. Now what does this mean and how is the utilitarian standard of maximization of the social good going to be applied to determine this? Rawls wants to claim that utilitarianism can be formulated in a way that makes the objection highly remote.[15]

Basic to his argument is the distinction between justifying a social institution (e.g., the institution of punishment) and justifying a particular action falling under it (e.g., a judge's sentencing someone to be punished). If the utilitarian standard is applied only to the justification of the institution of punishment which authorizes the judge's particular actions, says Rawls, then it is very unlikely that the utilitarian will end up justifying the framing of an innocent man. For what is the institution the utilitarian wishes to justify? It is a set of rules that authorize

14 Ted Honderich, *Punishment: The Supposed Justifications* (Harmondsworth, England: Penguin Books Ltd., 1971), p. 64.

15 John Rawls, "Two Concepts of Rules," *Philosophical Rev.,* 64 (1955), 3–32.

depriving someone of certain of his rights when he has violated a law, this being determined by a trial that follows due process, the law in question being strictly construed and on the books prior to the offense, etc. These features, taken together, characterize the institution of punishment. Now this institution might be compared with some other institution, called "telishment" by Rawls, which allows officials to frame an innocent man when they believe it would be in the interests of society. Clearly, telishment is open to much abuse and will be a source of insecurity on the part of the public, for it will never be known whom it is going to strike next. It is rather doubtful, says Rawls, that such an institution could be justified on utilitarian grounds and, therefore, it is not too realistically imaginable that framing an innocent person would ever be endorsed by the utilitarian-deterrence theory.

Rawls' formulation goes a long way toward answering the objection, but it is difficult to say whether it answers it completely. Rawls may be exaggerating the degree of insecurity that would be felt under a system of telishment (which does not rule out the use of punishment), especially if the system succeeds in reducing crime. In any case, the retributivist still seems to have the last word here. The permissibility of framing an innocent man is just one of the faults of the utilitarian-deterrence theory. It is possible to have an institution that does not allow official discretion and yet results in punishing persons known to be innocent. This would be the case if the penal law specified that for certain offenses the punishment should be inflicted on the offender's minor child, the violation being determined by a trial that follows due process, etc. Such punishments (and threats of punishment) might be highly effective as deterrents. This institution is not at all like telishment, and it is not nearly so doubtful that it could be justified on utilitarian grounds. Rawls, if he wishes, may refuse to call what occurs under this institution "punishment," but this really makes no difference. It appears in the end that the utilitarian-deterrence theory does justify "too much" and that the objection against it still holds.

I think we must conclude that the utilitarian-deterrence approach, in the versions we have considered, does not supply a morally acceptable justification of punishment. This conclusion, however, is highly disconcerting, for it seems most unreasonable to deny the relevance of deterrence to this problem. But there may be a way out of the difficulty if we follow Hart's contention, mentioned near the beginning of the chapter, that the problem of punishment is not a unitary issue but has several separable aspects. Thus we might say that utilitarian-deterrence answers the question of the general purpose of punishment, that is, of having any penal law at all. At the very least, forward-looking utilitarian-deterrence is a good reason for declaring certain acts to be punishable offenses. As to the questions of "Who?" and "How much?" utilitarian-deterrence needs to be supplemented (and limited) by principles of justice which are dear to retributivists. This solution to the difficulty has great appeal and is now widely accepted—yet it is doubtful that it can be adopted by a consistent utilitarian.[16]

Retribution, on the other hand, does not appear to be the answer as to why punishable offenses are created by law. Something is made a crime because we wish to deter people from committing it, not because we want to punish for it. Now retributivists might argue that this is not entirely correct regarding acts which are morally wrong, but we do not need to go into this now. It is enough to notice that retributivists are basically concerned with the justifiability of *inflicting* punishment. Let us turn to an examination of retributivism in its own right.

---

[16] A variety of utilitarianism we have not considered here is so-called Ideal Utilitarianism, which holds that the general happiness is only one good among many. My reason for not discussing it is that it is often assimilated to a retributivist theory of punishment.

CHAPTER FIVE

Punishment: Retributivism

RETRIBUTIVISM   Retributivism, by and large, has had a bad press. The very term connotes retaliation and revenge. Some opponents of the position go so far as to call it the "vindictive" theory, a theory that believes in pain for pain's sake. Two figures of speech current in retributivist literature are that the criminal has a "debt to pay" to society and that society "pays back" the criminal for his wrongdoing—tit for tat. Utilitarians argue that whereas their view is forward-looking and conceives punishment as a means to an end, retributivism easily degenerates into a cover for base feelings of vengefulness: when one is struck one wishes to strike back; when one is hurt one wishes to hurt in return, but to what purpose? Retributive punishment is bound to ignore both the needs of the offender and the needs of society. Modern opponents of punishment find the retributivist's backward-looking emphasis on guilt and blameworthiness especially outmoded and based upon an outdated psychology. Criminality should be treated as a disease, not requited with punishment, they say.

After all this, one may wonder whether there is anything that can be said in favor of retributivism. We are already familiar with its main contentions. It is wrong, unjust, to punish the innocent even when it would be socially useful to do so. This implies a close connection between punishment and desert, which also finds expression in the view that there should be a moral fit between the amount of punishment and the crime. Although these contentions are deeply ingrained in our ordinary, and perhaps uncritical, moral consciousness, the historical fact is that retributivists have disagreed on some basic points concerning the connection between punishment and desert.

In its classical form, represented by Immanuel Kant, retributivism maintains a *maximalist* position. This holds not merely that only the guilty should be punished, but also that there is a *duty* to punish someone who is guilty and culpable, which means that the individual has broken the law under conditions that characterize his illegal act or omission as blameworthy—i.e., he has no justification or excuse. Such a person is *deserving* of punishment, and there is a duty to punish him. A criminal should not be let off free. Maximalists hold, therefore, that criminals should be punished whether or not crime is thereby reduced—and presumably even if crime is thereby increased!

Most contemporary retributivists, on the other hand, maintain a *minimalist* position. This holds only that no one should be punished *unless* he is guilty of a crime and culpable. Culpable guilt is a morally necessary condition of punishment; one should be punished only if he deserves it. The fact that someone is deserving of punishment, however, does not necessarily mean that he should be punished. Minimalism allows a judge to absolve (partly or completely) an offender from punishment under certain conditions; e.g., when it would not serve the purposes of rehabilitation or deterrence (particular or general). Minimalist retributivism is usually combined with teleological considerations into a "pluralist" rationale for the infliction of punishment.[1]

Clearly, then, if a penal system were to be constructed along retributivist lines, the result would depend on the kind of retributivism adopted, although neither would permit punishing the innocent. A problem common to both is how society should handle (a) individuals who are "dangerous" (e.g., paranoids with violent tendencies) but have not yet committed a crime and (b) nonresponsible (and hence non-blameable) individuals who have committed a crime. Such persons might need to be restrained (in effect, imprisoned), but can retributivism allow this?

Another basic point of disagreement among retributivists, which also

---

[1] "Pluralism" should not be confused with utilitarian-deterrence theories which also reject punishment of the innocent. For them, this rejection is a matter of utilitarian efficiency or definition, not one of adherence to a principle of justice that has an independent moral status.

has implications for the sentencing policy of a penal system, concerns the amount of punishment. Retributivists assume that wrongful acts and harms can be ranked in order of their moral gravity and that punishments can be ranked in accordance with their severity. Now, although they accept the idea of a moral fit between punishment and offense, they differ on how this fit is to be measured. On this there are two main types of position:

1. The severity of a punishment should be *equal* in degree to the gravity of the act or harm done; e.g., the loss imposed on the offender should equal the loss suffered by the victim. This does not necessarily mean that the offender should suffer the identically same harm.
2. The severity of a punishment should be fixed in *relation* to the comparative gravity of the act or harm done, but not necessarily in an amount equal to it. This means that offenses of the same gravity should be punished in amounts that are equal to each other in severity and that offenses of different gravity should be punished in unequal amounts, with the graver offenses being punished more severely.

There are also two variants of these positions, which depend on whether or not the moral gravity of an act or harm is also, for purposes of punishment, considered a function of the degree of culpability of the agent. Generally, it is so considered. It should be noted that for minimalist retributivists the above yardsticks can be used only to set a criminal's maximum punishment. All retributivists agree, at least verbally, that no one should be punished more severely than he deserves.

It can be argued, with the best case going to "relational" minimalists, that the law to some extent reflects retributivist positions on the degree of punishment that should be assigned to an offense. For example, attempted murder is ordinarily punished less severely than murder, and negligent homicide less severely than premeditated homicide. (If deterrence—or the wickedness of the perpetrator's intention—were the only consideration, there would seem to be no reason for punishing an attempt any less severely than the completed crime.) Modern codes do grade offenses and accordingly attach maximum penalties to them. (The degree of culpability is usually an element in the definition of an offense and affects its grade.) We shall shortly consider some difficulties in the above positions. A problem common to them is how society should handle the so-called habitual criminal. He might need to be restrained for a longer period than would otherwise be merited for his current conviction (preventive detention). But can retributivism allow this?

Given this disunity among retributivists, it becomes all the more important to inquire into the theory's underlying basis. We should begin by recognizing that for retributivists, punishment is neither mere infliction of pain or loss on wrongdoers, nor, of course, something that is adopted because it "works." Rather, the act of punishing is an expression of a moral attitude. This idea, as Herbert Morris suggests, apparently has its origin in one's reaction to one's own wrongdoing.[2] In such circumstances one feels guilt or shame, and these feelings are experienced as painful or unpleasant. One feels remorseful and seeks forgiveness, desires to atone and "make it up." These actions serve to restore the relationship or condition that existed prior to the wrong act. A wrongdoer cannot simply let bygones be bygones. Although feelings of guilt or shame can have pathological manifestations, the capacity to have them is an ingredient of a morally healthy personality. A person who does wrong and does not as a consequence experience self-condemnation and its accompaniments will be regarded as morally deficient or even depraved. Now these inner reactions have their parallel in punishment. Punishment is society's reproachful response to crime. More than that, it is the emphatic denunciation of a crime, as Lord Denning says.

But it is precisely here that opponents of retributivism would insist on caution. For it is one thing to recognize the moral character of an individual's reaction to his own wrongdoing, but quite another to transfer this to someone else's (even society's) response to the individual's act. The dangers inherent in making this transfer are most evident in the case in which an injured party strikes back at the person who caused the hurt. Although the former may well rationalize and "moralize" this in the way just suggested (after all, the latter "had it coming to him"), it is often clear that the blow returned is basically the expression of a desire to cause pain and to receive satisfaction in so doing. This is vengeance—pain returned for pain caused—and only through self-deception can one view it otherwise. The same appears true at the social level, in the infliction of legal punishment. Unless it be for purposes of correction or deterrence, punishment is hostility toward the criminal as an enemy of society. As much is admitted by Justice Stephen, whose position has been classified as retributivistic. "The criminal law," according to Stephen, "regulates, sanctions, and provides a legitimate satisfaction for the passion of revenge; the criminal law stands to the passion of revenge in much the same relation as marriage to the sexual appetite."[3] Now, desire for revenge is a natural, human desire—as the saying goes, revenge is the best way to get even—but it hardly provides a moral justification for legal punishment any more than it does for "lynch law."

An interesting addition to this kind of argument is made by Honderich. He maintains that "the fact, *taken entirely by itself,* that a man has

2 "Guilt and Suffering," *Philosophy East and West,* 21 (1971), 419–34.

3 James Fitzjames Stephen, *A General View of the Criminal Law of England,* 2nd ed. (London: Macmillan, 1890), p. 99. Because this conceives of punishment as an institutionalized substitute for vengeance, some writers have classified Stephen's position as ultilitarian or teleological, at least. In any case, Stephen accepts the retributivisitic sounding notion that it is morally right to "hate" criminals.

caused a certain harm by a responsible action, seems to have no moral consequences." [4] By this he means that it cannot be connected with any recognizably moral attitude, and therefore does not provide a moral reason for action at all, good or bad. Why not? When someone is intentionally injured he has a grievance, and he receives a certain satisfaction when his assailant is punished. This satisfaction is described as "retaliatory" or "vindictive," and a similar satisfaction is experienced by others when the assailant is punished. But this vindictive response "cannot be regarded as generating a moral argument." [5]

Retributivists will quite rightly, I think, resist these attempts to reduce their conception of punishment to vengeance, for there are significant differences between the two. Vengeance is wreaked until satisfaction is given to outraged sentiments; retributive punishment has a presumably objective maximum. Secondly, an individual's response to being injured need not be completely vindictive, because his grievance may be justified. And even so, thirdly, the response of *others* to this situation might not be vindictive at all. (In fact, it may be semantically improper to describe their response as vindictive.) Consider the parallel case of social injustice. The demands of oppressed persons for redress of their grievances may well involve envy, and they might receive a certain satisfaction vis-à-vis their oppressors when the situation is rectified, a satisfaction not unlike the vindictive (but, so what?). But the demands of others that the oppressed should be given justice are expressions of *moral indignation,* which is a disinterested, not a self-centered, sentiment. (Moral indignation, however, is often dangerously mixed with unjustified feelings of self-righteousness.) This of course does not mean that these others receive no satisfaction in seeing the injustice rectified.

As for vengeance and punishment, both may involve hostility toward the malefactor; but while vengeance *aims* at personal satisfaction, punishment, at least in part, and perhaps wholly, is expressive of moral indignation. Of course, both can be misdirected. But here the retributivist insists that punishment should be inflicted only on the culpably guilty, lest a grave injustice be done to the one who receives its brunt. Although caution is obviously called for in reacting to wrongdoing,[6] the con-

---

[4] Ted Honderich, *Punishment: The Supposed Justifications* (Harmondsworth, England: Penguin Books Ltd., 1971), p. 44; italics in original.

[5] Ibid., p. 83. It seems to me that Honderich's attempt to reduce retributive punishment to satisfactions fails in the case of attempts or conspiracies to commit crimes (where there is no injured party) and in the case of murder (where the victim cannot receive vindictive satisfaction).

[6] "No punishment, no matter from whom it comes, may be inflicted out of hatred. Hence men have a duty to cultivate a *conciliatory spirit*. But this must not be confused with *placid toleration* of injuries, renunciation of the rigorous means for preventing the recurrence of injuries by other men; for in the latter case a man would be throwing

demnatory response to it *can* be connected to a recognizably moral attitude.

But need this condemnation take the form of inflicting pain or loss? This is Professor Joel Feinberg's question. Punishment, he maintains, has in fact two separable aspects: hard treatment and symbolic condemnation. It is in virtue of the latter aspect that punishment enables us to disavow a crime or to absolve others from suspicion of guilt. At the present time, hard treatment is a *conventional* way of expressing reprobation, but Feinberg speculates whether this condemnatory function couldn't as well be achieved by a dramatic public ritual—the more heinous the crime, the more dramatic and shaming the ritual, presumably, for justice demands that the condemnatory aspect (but not the hard treatment) should fit the crime.[7]

I find it difficult to assess this intriguing argument, for it is not clear to me that the two aspects of punishment are as separable as Feinberg thinks. Retributive punishment—punishment meted out because it is deserved—always signifies some degree of condemnation, but we can strongly condemn without doing anything that could be called punishing. Secondly, even if, as Feinberg holds, not all "penalties" are punitive, punishing does seem to involve penalizing. It is also difficult to determine whether his speculations establish that punishment can completely dispense with the element of pain or loss (except, of course, that which is incidental to the ritual). It is true that the ignominy of a criminal conviction is sometimes regarded as sufficient punishment for an offender, and this leads the judge to remit or lighten the sentence. In serious cases, I suppose, a criminal could be branded—under anaesthesia, naturally—and he would thus carry his mark of infamy for the rest of his life. It is not at all obvious that the consequences of this, or some other dramatic ritual, would be any lighter for him than the hard treatment of conventional imprisonment. Very dramatic rituals of condemnation might also lead to demands for harsher treatment of criminals.

Be this as it may, Feinberg's argument, as he indicates, does throw into question a variety of retributivism that dispenses with notions of condemnation or vengeance and that sees the ultimate justifying purpose of punishment as making the offender suffer in an amount equal to his crime. Now, there are difficulties in this "equalizer" position, but I doubt that retributivists ever do entirely dispense with the notion of condemnation. Whatever its ultimate justification, retributive punishment expresses a condemnatory attitude toward wrongdoing.

---

away his right and letting others trample on it...." Immanuel Kant, *The Doctrine of Virtue: Part II of the Metaphysic of Morals*, trans. M. J. Gregor (New York: Harper Torchbooks, 1964), p. 130.

7 Joel Feinberg, *Doing and Deserving* (Princeton: Princeton University Press, 1970), Chapter 5 ("The Expressive Function of Punishment").

MAXIMAL
RETRIBUTIVISM:
KANT

With this background we can now turn to a positive account and examination of the doctrine of Immanuel Kant, who is the paragon of classical retributivists. Many writers in fact identify retributivism with his view. Kant maintained both the maximalist position that there is a duty to punish someone who is culpably guilty of having committed a crime and the position that the punishment should equal the gravity of the offense. The following quotation gives the flavor of his theory:

> If someone has committed a murder, he must die. . . . Even if a civil society were to dissolve itself by common agreement of all its members (for example, if the people inhabiting an island decided to separate and disperse themselves around the world), the last murderer remaining in prison must first be executed, so that everyone will duly receive what his actions are worth and so that the bloodguilt thereof will not be fixed on the people because they failed to insist on carrying out the punishment; for if they fail to do so, they may be regarded as accomplices in this public violation of legal justice.[8]

This makes it quite clear that forward-looking considerations, such as deterrence and reform, are quite irrelevant to whether and how much punishment ought to be inflicted on a lawbreaker.

But why, then should he be punished? In order to understand Kant's maximalism, we need to take a brief look at his view of law and legal justice. The keynote of Kant's thought is the idea of *freedom,* and one of his main problems is to determine the limits of freedom and the conditions under which coercion is justified. Punishment is in fact characterized as a "one-sided use of coercion" in which a man's sense of honor and dignity as a free being is hurt.

According to Kant, the concepts of law, justice, and rights analytically entail an authorization to use coercion. As free beings, men have the right to realize their freedom in action. This in turn requires that each should in his actions respect the rights of others, for no one can in fairness claim a right to act on the basis of his own free choice unless he concedes a similar right to others. Rights, we may say, are a person's legitimate freedoms. Now if it were the case that everything people did in no way impeded the freedom of others, there would be no problem posed for us; but this is clearly not the case. There is, therefore, a need for general laws which accord with principles of fairness and which thereby enable the legitimate freedoms of one person to "coexist" with those of others. Justice, says Kant, is the "aggregate of those conditions under which the will of one person can be conjoined with the will of another in accordance with a universal law." [9] Juridical laws are, by their very nature, coercive limitations on freedom.

[8] Immanuel Kant, *The Metaphysical Elements of Justice,* trans. John Ladd (Indianapolis: Bobbs-Merrill, 1965), p. 102.

[9] Ibid., p. 34.

Now, according to Kant, an act is "just" in a strict sense if—irrespective of the motive behind it—it is consistent with such laws, and "unjust" if it is inconsistent with them. An unjust act is a violation of the rights of others, and hence, we may say, it is morally wrong. Coercion under the conditions of law in order to prevent a breach of rights, on the other hand, is morally right. Such coercion is a "hindrance to a hindrance" of legitimate freedom and is therefore justifiable. Freedom is limited for the sake of freedom itself. It is clear that Kant's doctrine, though nonutilitarian, is not entirely nonteleological. Furthermore, Kant apparently accepts the idea that laws serve a *deterrent* purpose because they contain the implied threat that coercion may be used to prevent breaches of them. This also comes out in his discussion of the so-called "right of necessity." If I kill an innocent person in order to save my own life (for example, I push you away from a life preserver to save myself from drowning), I have done something which is clearly morally wrong and unjust. Nevertheless, Kant thinks that I should be excused from punishment because the threat of it could not have psychologically operated on me at the time.

On Kant's theory, then, each person can be obliged—i.e., forced— to obey the law. But each person also has an obligation to obey the law. This is conceived by Kant as a *debt* which is *owed* to others. Laws secure rights; my freedom is restricted for the sake of yours and yours for the sake of mine. The obligation or debt is therefore reciprocal. We have rights against each other and owe it to each other to obey the law. There is, therefore, the possibility of reciprocal coercion, for law, justice, and rights mean the same as an "authorization to use coercion." This does not mean, however, that the individual is necessarily authorized to use coercion when his rights are threatened. The situation of "distributive legal justice," rights under law, can be attained only in civil society; otherwise every man would be the judge of his own cause. Only legally constituted authority, which presumably operates in accordance with the rule of law, may actually use this coercion. Kant holds that there is a moral duty to enter civil society because we have a duty to secure justice and the respect of rights in action.

Proceeding now to punishment, it might be thought that the next logical step for Kant is to espouse a deterrence justification of it, for he apparently maintains that law not only specifies the ground rules of just action but also serves a preventive function. In fact, Kant allows that there is a kind of punishment which is pragmatic and utilitarian and which is based upon what experience has shown to be the most effective means of preventing crime.[10] But Kant will have none of this. First of all, it has nothing to do with the *justice* of the punishment and it is not a moral justification at all. (The latter point seems excessively

---

[10] Ibid., p. 132, n. 3. In the precritical *Lectures on Ethics,* trans. L. Infield (New York: Harper Torchbooks, 1963; p. 55), Kant states that "all punishments imposed by sovereigns and governments are pragmatic."

narrow to me.) Just punishment is always retributive, imposed because one is culpably guilty of having committed a crime. Secondly, a deterrence justification opens the door to all sorts of perversions of justice. It permits both the punishment of the innocent and the exemption of the guilty. We must avoid the "winding paths" of utilitarianism like the plague.

In order for someone to be justly punished, according to Kant, a court must first find him guilty and culpable. This means not only that he broke the law but also that he was responsible for his criminal act; i.e., it can be imputed to him as his own. Furthermore, it means that the individual knowingly broke the law—was aware that his act was unlawful. (This sets the standard of culpability quite high, higher than in most legal systems.) A person who has thus committed a crime acquires *moral demerit,* the legal effect of which is punishment. There are, however, degrees of culpability, depending on the extent of imputability of the act. An act committed under emotional stress, for example, is less culpable, has lesser demerit, than one done in cool deliberation. This is an important consideration for sentencing purposes.

We can now see why Kant maintains that it is unjust to punish the innocent and just to punish the criminal. These are not mere matters of moral intuition but are consequent upon his theory of rights, justice, and law. Punishment is a one-sided use of coercion and involves a deprivation of at least some rights. Now, we owe it to a person to respect his rights in our actions as he owes it to us in his. But punishing an innocent person—that is, a person who stayed within the bounds of legitimate freedom—is manifestly a violation of this reciprocal debt: it is a violation of justice and unfair to him. Justice requires that persons be treated equally in regard to their rights unless there are morally relevant differences between them.

On the other side, a crime exceeds the perpetrator's legitimate freedom and infringes on the rights of others, regarding which he owes the debt of respect in action. In knowingly breaking the law, the criminal in effect declares that he has a license to steal, for example, and he puts everyone who would respect property rights at a disadvantage. The criminal weakens the fabric of justice. He *must* be punished in order to vindicate justice and rights. He should not be allowed to profit from his wrong-doing. (Condemnation, by itself, is insufficient.) Failure to punish is not only condonation of unjust acts—in effect, a declaration of their permissibility—but is also unfair to those who practice self-restraint and respect the rights of others in their actions. This idea underlies our speaking of a debt that the criminal has to pay to society. In a sense, the law provides a kind of "pricing system." It says that if one wishes to commit a crime, one must pay a certain price for it. This does not mean, however, that one has permission to commit crimes as long as he is willing to pay the price. Crimes are moral wrongs and they deserve punishment. It is not correct to say, as some opponents do, that retributive punishment is pain for pain's sake. It is imposed for the sake of justice.[11]

The above account, I think, embodies the main lines of the theory behind Kant's maximalism. Crucial to it is the conception of crime as a violation of rights. It should be noted, however, that Kant also recognizes certain "unnatural crimes," including rape and other acts of sexual indecency, some of which cannot easily be fitted under the aforementioned conception. In a way, he seems to regard such "unnatural crimes" as even more deserving of punishment, for he views them as crimes against humanity, as degrading to the human element. One who commits bestiality, for example, shows himself to be unworthy to remain in human society (which provides, perhaps, a way for linking these crimes to the general conception), and should be permanently exiled from it. But if we stick to the main lines of Kant's theory, at any rate, some of the standard objections to retributivism can be answered.

**OBJECTIONS
TO RETRIBUTIVISM** Retributivism is the position that it is right to punish a criminal irrespective of any future benefits which might thereby accrue to him or to others. Now this, it is argued, can only rest upon the alleged moral intuition that it is fitting, right in itself, that the culpably guilty should be made to suffer. But appeals to intuition are notoriously unsatisfactory. Moreover, to say that punishment is right in itself is not to offer a reason for it, for one is in effect denying that a reason is at all necessary.

This objection does not hold water as far as Kant is concerned. It is true that Kant holds that punishing the culpably guilty is right in itself, but this is not based upon mere moral intuition, as we saw; rather, it is based upon his analysis of law, rights, and justice. Kant does offer reasons for the intrinsic rightness of punishing, and he would see nothing improper with this procedure from his point of view. The objection, however, appears to assume that all genuine "reasons" are necessarily forward looking, which begs the question as against retributivism. At issue here are opposed conceptions of morality and moral reasoning.

Another objection goes as follows. Retributivism maintains that culpable offenders should be punished because a violation of law is also a moral wrong, and we have a duty to punish moral wrongdoing. But this is incorrect. No one (except God) has the right, let alone the duty, to

[11] See C. W. K. Mundle, "Punishment and Desert," *Philosophical Quarterly,* 4 (1954), 216–28.

punish moral wrongdoing as such. There is no moral penal law. If I make a "lying promise" to meet you for lunch next Tuesday, I've committed a moral wrong. No one but you is in a position to forgive me for the inconvenience I caused you when you relied on my promise; but not even you are in a position to punish me for my moral misbehavior. No one is authorized to punish for moral wrongs. (It is not even always proper to castigate the wrongdoer to his face.)

Again, the answer to this objection is to be found in the main lines of Kant's theory. The moral wrongs in question are violations of rights, and rights carry an authorization to use coercion. We punish in vindication of rights, and a right to punish is held by the judicial organs of civil society, which we have a moral duty to enter.

Interestingly enough, the above objection has been raised not only by opponents of retributivism but also by Mabbott, who is himself a retributivist. In an important article, Mabbott presents a *legalistic* variety of retributivism.[12] He claims that just as one cannot forgive moral evil (although one can forgive personal injury), one cannot punish moral evil. We can, however, punish violations of laws. Like some revisionist utilitarians, Mabbott maintains that the decision to have any rules at all, and which rules to have, is utilitarian; but the acceptance of a legal system entails surrendering utilitarian considerations in applying the rules to particular cases. The imposition of punishment should be determined by the past fact of the criminal's having broken the law. In breaking the law the criminal brings his punishment on himself, says Mabbott. Now, Kant fully agrees with this last statement, but he would object to Mabbott's severing of punishment from morality. How can we say that a lawbreaker is morally—and not just legally—deserving of punishment unless his act is also morally wrong in some sense? After all, the retributive theory is supposed to be a moral justification of punishment, in fact, of its justness.

It is appropriate, in passing, to at least raise the question of how far Kant meant his maximalist doctrine to apply to actual legal systems. Does Kant think that a person who knowingly breaks *any* positive law of his society deserves to be punished? (This should not be confused with the issue of the justness of the particular punishments imposed.) To put this more sharply, suppose the law in question is itself unjust, i.e., its specification of rights is not in accordance with principles of fairness. Is punishment warranted in such a case? If I understand him correctly, Kant's answer, rather surprisingly, is Yes; for he apparently holds that we have an obligation to obey the positive laws even if they are unjust or bad although we can try to bring about their repeal. Further discussion of this topic would take us into Kant's political philosophy.

[12] J. D. Mabbott, "Punishment," *Mind,* 49 (1939), 152–67.

Our last objections to maximalist retributivism may now be considered. The first of these, it seems to me, is quite serious, and it is not one for which Kant has a ready answer at all. It is that in inflicting punishment on the culpable offender, other individuals—innocent individuals—are also likely to be made to suffer. That "reflex stroke" (as some retributivists are wont to call it) of retributive punishment can strike not only the criminal but also his relatives and dependents, and may deprive them of needed support. But it is prima facie wrong knowingly to inflict suffering on innocent individuals. Such suffering also constitutes a deprivation of rights to which these persons are entitled. Now this suffering is something of which the utilitarian-deterrence theorist can take account in determining what acts to criminalize and when and how much to punish. He can also figure into his calculations the financial and social costs of operating the penal system at large. Basically, the utilitarian-deterrence theorist views it as an unfortunate fact that we have to punish at all. We punish in order to reduce the total incidence of harm in society, and for this a certain price is paid. But where the costs are too high, punishment should not be resorted to.

It is hard to see what reply the maximalist can give to this objection. Justice requires that certain acts (infringements of rights) be treated as criminal wrongs and that punishment be meted out for them. A society that fails to punish the culpably guilty is in violation of a duty of justice. And, as Kant says in precisely this connection, "If legal justice perishes, then it is no longer worth while for men to remain on this earth." [13] Lawbreakers, then, must be punished. But even if we grant that the "evil" imposed on them is completely justifiable, we can hardly say the same about the suffering and deprivation of rights experienced by the innocent (unless it be on utilitarian grounds). The only solution to this difficulty that I can find for the maximalist is that the system of criminal justice should be so designed as to result in no suffering for those others who are adversely affected by the punishing of the criminal, but this seems totally unrealistic. The maximalist might also be tempted to say that the suffering experienced by the innocent is unintended and, therefore, morally acceptable, but this is evasive. It is clear that the justice that is meted out in punishment will be *rough justice*. (This is also the case because legal systems operate inefficiently and arbitrarily to some extent.) In that case there is no reason why the imposition of punishment should be guided solely by maximalist considerations, although one can still hold that the culpably guilty are deserving of punishment. The above objection militates a shift at least toward the minimalist position; namely, that no one should be punished *unless* he deserves it.

Finally, it can be argued that the adoption of maximalism will not

[13] *The Metaphysical Elements of Justice,* p. 100.

necessarily satisfy either the needs of society or the needs of the offender. Crime is a social problem of many dimensions and the punitive approach to it is not always the most appropriate. As for the offender, it will often, and perhaps always, be more advisable to adopt the nonpunitive orientation that is now common in connection with juveniles. Now, the first part of this twofold objection raises issues which are too complex for discussion here. I do not think that it shows that retribution should not be a factor in punishment, but it nevertheless suggests that maximalism, the duty to punish, needs to be weighed in the balance with other considerations. Penal justice, in Kant's narrow sense, is only one value among many, and other social interests are also of relevance to the ethics of punishment. The second aspect of the objection will be taken up shortly in our discussion of modern rejections of punishment.

HOW MUCH PUNISHMENT? We turn now to the issue of the *amount* of punishment that should be meted out for a crime. On the Kantian, classical retributivist view this is entirely a question of justice, not deterrent efficiency. A just amount of punishment is the amount deserved, merited because of the nature of the offense, and according to Kant the measure of just punishment is *equality*: the severity of the punishment should equal the moral gravity of the offense (which is, apparently, a function both of the unlawful act and the degree of the offender's culpability). This is in the "spirit" of the *lex talionis* ("an eye for an eye"). It is important to note that although the questions of the rightfulness of punishment and of the just amount of punishment are distinct, many writers do not treat them separately. Kant seems to have been one of these. Presumably, if there is a duty to punish all criminals in an amount equal to their crime, there is a duty to punish all criminals.

A standard argument for this equalizing position appeals to the ancient notions of universal justice and the moral governance of the universe. A universe in which virtue and happiness are combined is of higher value than one in which vice and happiness are combined. In a just and perfect world, happiness would be distributed in exact proportion to a person's moral worth.[14] Now when a person does wrong and acquires moral demerit, his accounts can be squared, his books balanced, so to speak, when he is made to suffer in an amount equal to his demerit. His punishment is like a "negative wage," the opposite of the rewarding payment he would have been entitled to had he acted meritoriously. In fact, the

[14] See Immanuel Kant, *Critique of Practical Reason*, trans. L. W. Beck (Chicago: University of Chicago Press, 1950), p. 215.

suffering or deprivation experienced by the wrongdoer is itself good, for "wickedness humbled and subdued" is better than "wickedness successful and triumphant." [15] When a wrongdoer is made to suffer in an amount equal in severity to the gravity of his deed, his punishment is not only just in relation to him but also restores the moral balance that existed prior to his wrongful act.

There is little doubt that something like the above argument is in the back of Kant's mind. Interestingly enough, however, he makes no explicit reference to it in his discussion of legal punishment in *The Metaphysical Elements of Justice*. There, his argument in favor of an equalizing standard is that it is the only objective, nonarbitrary yardstick we can use. It provides for consistency and fairness of disposition among wrongdoers, because each person who commits an offense of a given grade can receive an equal, if not identical, treatment. All other measures are bound to be wavering and arbitrary. The objective fairness of the equalizing standard is also immediately recognizable. When someone is punished in this degree he has no cause for complaint, which he would have if the severity exceeded the gravity of the crime. So also would others in the society have cause for complaint if the severity were less than the gravity of his offense. Justice is vindicated when punishment and offense are equal.

It is unnecessary to examine the cogency of these arguments, for the equalizing measure is unworkable in the context of legal punishment. It is one thing to say that a person who causes injury should pay a sum equal to the damage—the *lex talionis* was already interpreted along this line in ancient times—but it is quite another to say that the severity of punishment should equal the moral gravity of the crime.

By what *units* shall we measure the wrongfulness of an unlawful act? By what units shall we measure an offender's culpability? Do these units measure the same kind of thing? How should they be combined, if this is considered necessary? By what units shall we measure the severity of a punishment, and are these units comparable to the units by which the gravity of the crime is measured? The answers to these questions are not forthcoming. As for apportioning happiness to a person's moral worth, this would involve us in humanly impossible calculations, as Sir David Ross points out, because a person's life as a whole must be taken into account. It could be the case that the person we are about to punish is already enjoying less happiness than a perfectly fair distribution would allow him. [16]

We must conclude, then, that the equalizing standard is unworkable.

[15] These phrases come from Hastings Rashdall, *The Theory of Good and Evil*, first published 1907 (Oxford: Oxford University Press, 1948), I, 294.

[16] W.D. Ross, *The Right and the Good* (Oxford: Clarendon Press, 1930), pp. 56–65.

In fairness, however, to Kant and other proponents, it should be said that it is not entirely certain how literally they mean "equality of amount" to be understood. What is important to Kant is the preservation of the "spirit" of the *lex talionis* as a measure of just punishment. In the case of homicide, he sees no equivalent alternative to the death penalty, but for other crimes the matter of literal equality is less clear. Kant insists, for example, that rape should be punished by castration. Obviously, there is no basis for saying that this punishment is literally equal in amount to this crime, although it may in some sense be the appropriate punishment for it. This suggests that we should consider whether the relational position supplies a more workable standard of just punishment. I think that it can help us to retain, to an extent, the retributivist notion of a "moral fit" between punishment and offense, but it needs considerable qualification. We cannot completely abandon this notion if we wish to hold on to the principle that no one should be punished more than he deserves.

The relational position maintains that an offender should be punished *relative* to the moral gravity of his crime; more serious offenses should be punished more severely than lesser offenses and crimes of equal gravity should be punished by equally severe penalties. This standard does not involve the use of "units" of gravity or severity, but it does presuppose the possibility of comparisons: more, equal, and less. Now it seems to me that we should probably give up the idea of one crime being equal in gravity to another, but I think that we can, and do, grade offenses on a series of rough scales. Although there is sure to be some disagreement, we still share the sense that certain harms and certain invasions of rights are more serious than others. We also make distinctions of culpability, taking into account the agent's complicity in the unlawful act, whether he acted with malice aforethought, negligently, under provocation, etc. The rough scales undoubtedly cannot be frozen for all times and circumstances, and at any given moment they should be as reasoned as possible.

We can also make scales in which punishments are ranked according to their severity. These, too, will be rough and all the more so if they include different kinds of penalties (e.g., corporal, imprisonment, and fines). We must recognize that the nominally same punishment (e.g., a $1,000 fine, a ten-year sentence) will affect people differently. When a given scale of punishments is coordinated with a scale of offenses, therefore, we should then think of these punishments as maximums, allowing for some flexibility in applying them to particular offenders.

Given a scale of penalties and a scale of offenses, we can now say that the more severe punishments should be imposed only for the more severe offenses and the lesser for the lesser. But this needs further qualification, for as it stands it could lead to injustice. Suppose the scale of penalties consisted of really draconian punishments, the least of which is ten years in jail. And suppose that the offense of loitering was ranked low on the given offense scale. We would hardly feel that justice is being done when a loiterer is sentenced to ten years. Such a penalty is excessive in relation to loitering (though not necessarily as a deterrent); it is more than is deserved. We must be prepared, therefore, to revise any scale of punishments in relation to a scale of offenses, and gradually work toward punishments that are roughly appropriate to a set of offenses. But we do need to start out with some scales, initially.

Assuming that this complicated task can be carried out, I think that the relational position supplies a standard of *rough justice* regarding the amount of punishment due for a crime, a rough "moral fit." There will be a good deal of overlap among the penalties for many crimes, especially for those near the center of our scales. But this is inevitable. The punishment that roughly fits a crime will not necessarily accord with what deterrence might require; it could be more, and it could be less severe. Nor will it necessarily accord with what strict justice, exact proportionality to moral blameworthiness, might require (this we must leave to God); again, it could be more, and it could be less severe. We will never be in a position to say that a criminal has been given exactly what he morally deserves. Nevertheless, a standard of rough justice, arguably, is better than no standard, because it at least sets a maximum to the amount of punishment. This is important as long as we still believe that no one should be punished in excess of his deserts, although we will often be doing this, unfortunately.

If the relational position is adopted, it is clear that the justice administered in punishment will be rough justice. This was also the conclusion of the discussion of maximalism. The question therefore arises whether these two pillars of retributivism together provide a morally acceptable basis for the institution and imposition of punishment. Shall justice, really rough justice, be done "though the heavens fall"? It can be argued that we ought not to give up trying to do rough justice—that is, having a system of laws which provide punishment for the commission of certain kinds of acts and imposing punishments in the relativistically determined amounts on as many culpably guilty lawbreakers as we can. All this is necessary in order to vindicate rights, to disavow crime, and to condemn wrongdoing. Otherwise, the criminal law loses whatever moral force it has.

I think there is some truth to these contentions, but given that it is rough justice that we are talking about, I do not see why the institution and administration of a retributivist system of "criminal justice" should not be qualified by utilitarian-deterrence considerations. These are undeniably relevant to the justification of having laws that threaten punishment (why punish at all?), and they are also relevant to the practical operation of the system, a system which involves the expenditure of social resources as well as costs to the innocent. Punishment based upon utilitarian-deterrence also provides a certain kind of justice insofar as it has the effect of protecting the rights and legitimate interests of many members of the community, even though it does not aim at securing punitive justice. But I do not think that we can totally abandon retributivism in favor of a thoroughgoing utilitarian-deterrence theory, if the objections earlier voiced against it have any validity. There is, however, another alternative—namely, that punishment itself should be abandoned as a means of dealing with crime. We shall consider, this shortly.

MINIMAL RETRIBUTIVISM

We shall now complete our discussion of retributivism by taking up the doctrine of *minimalism*. This maintains that no one ought to be punished unless he is culpably guilty of a crime. As mentioned, this principle is endorsed by all retributivists. Thus, Kant states:

> A human being can never be manipulated merely as a means to the purposes of someone else.... His innate personality [that is, his right as a person] protects him against such treatment, even though he may indeed be condemned to lose his civil personality. He must first be found deserving of punishment before any consideration is given to the utility of this punishment for himself or for his fellow citizens.[17]

Maximalists go on to say that we should punish all those who are culpably guilty. This is what minimalists reject. They are basically concerned to rule out the permissibility of punishing the innocent, and this they do on grounds of justice and not for the reasons offered by revisionist utilitarians. It is unfair to single out someone and make him suffer or be deprived of the ordinary rights of citizens unless he is culpably guilty of breaking the law.

If the utilitarian-deterrence theory appears to justify "too much" (the permissibility of punishing the innocent), it can be argued that the minimalist principle justifies "too little"; that is, it disallows depriving certain people of their rights, particularly their liberty, when there may be good reason for doing so. The hard problem for the retributivist arises in the case of persons who have not committed a crime but who pose a danger to themselves or to others and who should therefore be confined to some kind of institution.

[17] Kant, *The Metaphysical Elements of Justice*, p. 100.

This in fact happens daily in numerous jurisdictions under the practice of *civil commitment*. A person who is deemed mentally ill and dangerous to himself or others may be involuntarily confined to a mental institution. Why wait until a paranoid goes berserk and kills somebody? Even if it be granted that it is unjust to the individual, it nevertheless seems justifiable to deprive him of his liberty in advance of his act. This seems no different from putting someone with smallpox into quarantine because he poses a danger to society. Why then should we wait until a dangerous person has broken the law before we can put him "inside"?

An upholder of the minimalist principle might want to deal with this problem by directly attacking the practice of civil commitment.[18] The person with smallpox *already* poses a danger to the public; an allegedly mentally ill person may or may not do wrong. Everyone wishes to be protected from smallpox and should therefore be as willing to submit to quarantine, when he is infected, as to subject others to it when they are. But all of us have a bad streak and anyone *might* do something wrong; yet no one would be willing to submit to prior restraint for this reason. Otherwise, we could end up as the king's messenger does in Lewis Carroll's *Through the Looking-Glass* (Chapter 5): the messenger is imprisoned not only before his trial but also before his crime. ("Suppose he never commits the crime?" said Alice. "That would be all the better, wouldn't it?" the Queen said.) As Thomas Szasz has argued, civil commitment is given to extraordinary abuse.[19] Numerous individuals are put away, often because of the selfish motives of others, on the basis of unobjective or vague criteria of mental illness and unfounded predictions of dangerousness. The potential for injustice is so great that deprivation of liberty should be allowed only regarding culpably guilty lawbreakers.

Is this response adequate? Almost, but not quite, I think. A system which allowed for the confinement of anyone who might do wrong would be intolerably unjust. (In fact, however, in many jurisdictions anyone may be involuntarily confined for observation on the mere say-so of a physician.) Civil commitment *is* open to tremendous abuse. But this perhaps only shows the need for procedural safeguards that will ensure that only those who are seriously disturbed and highly likely to do something harmful will be involuntarily committed. A problem similar to this also arises under "preventive detention" as practiced in some jurisdictions. On grounds of anticipated danger, certain persons accused of crimes may be denied pretrial release. An ounce of detention is worth a pound of cure. Plainly, this is also open to abuse and may be a source of injustice. But

[18] He might also be tempted to reply with something like the "definitional stop": civil commitment is not punishment, and we are only concerned with who may be punished. But this would be the wrong answer, I think, because the moral issue of punishment, for the retributivist, is that of the justice of imposing suffering or loss of ordinary rights.

[19] *Law, Liberty and Psychiatry* (New York: The Macmillan Company, 1963).

again, perhaps more stringent safeguards are required to prevent excesses. I do not think that either civil commitment or preventive detention can be completely ruled out if there are adequate safeguards against abuses. The potential victims of genuinely dangerous people are also entitled to protection.

It is obvious that the doctrine of minimalism, by itself, is deficient as a theory of punishment. At most, it tells us that an offender should never be punished merely for deterrent or rehabilitative purposes but also to vindicate justice by giving him what he deserves, that retribution is always an element in justified punishment. (In any given instance, however, it is almost impossible to tell *why* someone is being punished.) Clearly, the minimalist position needs to be supplemented by other principles in order to determine specifically who shall be punished and who shall be exempted from punishment. A major problem here is ensuring the fair and even-handed administration of punishment.

But it also seems to me that none of the theories we have considered—utilitarian-deterrence, maximalist retributivism—can stand alone. We need some kind of *pluralistic* theory of punishment, and by this I do not mean a theory which, for example, merely holds (a) that utilitarian-deterrence is the answer to "Why punish at all?" (b) that retributivism of some sort answers to "Whom shall we punish?" and (c) that retributivism of some sort (or utilitarian-deterrence) answers to "How much punishment?" We need a more complex pluralism because, I think, both retributivist and deterrence considerations are relevant to all these points. In any case, no one has done for pluralism the kind of detailed job that Bentham did in working out the classical deterrence theory. It is not yet clear that an ethically consistent pluralism is possible.

SHOULD PUNISHMENT BE ABOLISHED? At the opening of this chapter I referred to modern skepticism regarding punishment. We shall now close with a brief discussion of the view which supports its *abolition*. This does not maintain that lawbreakers should go scot-free, but rather that they should be dealt with in a nonpunitive fashion. Proponents of this position are highly doubtful of the deterrent value of punishment. Most of all, they are impressed by the extraordinary rate of recidivism and draw the conclusion that punishment itself is at fault. The appropriate response to crime, they say, is *treatment,* where this is feasible. This position is an extension of earlier trends toward the "individualization" of punishment, the idea that punishment should be adjusted to the rehabilitative "needs" of the offender rather than to his deserts. Abolitionists assume that the more rehabilitative and therapeutic our approach, the less punitive we are in our dealings with the offender, because they take punishment to be equivalent to a kind of vindictive retributivism.

A leading and exceptionally cautious defender of the abolition of punishment is the sociologist and social worker Lady Barbara Wooton. Most of her argument turns upon the complex issue of responsibility. Although we have not gone into this topic, the main outlines of her argument can nevertheless be presented. It starts with the fact that modern legal systems contain highly developed doctrines whereby responsible offenders are distinguished from the nonresponsible and whereby various excuses and defenses (e.g., insanity) will relieve someone from liability to punishment. Most people grant that certain mentally ill offenders should not be punished; if anything, they should be sent to hospitals.[20]

Now, on the basis of a close analysis, Wooton argues that there is no absolute distinction between mentally ill and mentally healthy offenders and that criteria of responsibility should be allowed to "wither away." The trial should be confined solely to whether the accused did in fact commit the offense. If this was indeed the case, the individual would then be turned over to a board of experts for a determination of the kind of treatment he needs. In some cases it might be decided that the offender can be released immediately; in others, that he is incurable and should be put under permanent supervision. In any event, there would be nothing like a "determinate sentence," for this Wooton regards as a relic of the outmoded retributivist notion that punishment must fit the crime. Rather, an offender should be detained until it is safe to return him to society—that is, until his treatment is completed. (In many cases treatment could be given under conditions of minimal supervision.) Under Wooton's proposal there would be important shifts in the processes of the criminal law and corrections: prosecutor, judge, and warden would be largely displaced by psychiatrist and social worker; the distinction between prison and mental hospital would substantially disappear. All this is held to be a consequence of an approach to crime which focuses upon the forward-looking purpose of preventing the recurrence of crime through treatment.[21]

Many aspects of this proposal call for comment. One of the most important is what is meant by "treatment." Many things can go under this

[20] An extreme and influential proponent of the abolition of punishment is the psychiatrist Karl Menninger. In *The Crime of Punishment* (New York: Viking Compass Book, 1972), Menninger maintains that crime is an "illness." I do not find any evidence presented for this, nor is it clear what it even means. For further discussion, see Edmund Pincoffs' contribution to *Punishment: For and Against* (New York: Hart Publishing Company, 1971), pp. 208–20.

[21] Barbara Wooton, *Social Science and Social Pathology* (London: George Allen & Unwin, 1959). For a critical discussion, see various articles in H. L. A. Hart's *Punishment and Responsibility*.

name: psychoanalysis, brain surgery, sterilization, electric shock, drug therapy, behavior modification or conditioning, "aversion" therapy (which is hard to distinguish from plain old-fashioned torture), occupational training, etc. Wooton is not specific on what she has in mind. Are we to say that anything done by a physician, psychologist, or social worker is by definition treatment? And is any kind of treatment morally acceptable as long as it has the effect of preventing the offender from recommitting his offense? There are, in fact, many schools of therapy, but Wooton does not indicate the criteria for selecting the board of experts who determine the treatment that the offenders should receive. She speaks of treatment adjusted to the "needs" of the offender, but this may be viewed differently by different schools. Moreover, the "needs" of the offender may be quite different from the "needs" of society. Is it the case that what is good for the offender is also necessarily good for society, and vice versa? As Herbert Packer says, we should be as suspicious of the urge to cure as of the urge to punish.

But let us put these and other questions aside and go immediately to the crux of the issue. Does all this medical-sounding talk of "treatment" really amount to the elimination of punishment or is it at bottom highly misleading? The issue may be put in Lady Wooton's own terms: can we "envisage a system in which sentence is not automatically equated with 'punishment' "? [22] I do not think we can.

The foremost point concerns what it means for a society to have a set of penal laws. (Wooton, in contrast to many other writers, is clear that her scheme retains penal laws.) Penal laws typically forbid (or require) the performance of certain acts and they contain *threats* of unwelcome consequences in the event of violations. As deterrence theorists have emphasized, the main purpose in having such laws and threats is to deter people from committing the undesired acts. It is most implausible to say that the main purpose in having penal laws is to rehabilitate offenders. Now, even if we were to substitute various treatments for the penalties currently on the books, most people would continue to regard the possibility of incurring these consequences as a good reason for conforming to the law. For most people, these potential consequences would still function as threats of punishment, and they would (and should) continue to call it punishment when the threat falls due.

Secondly, most offenders will surely realize that they are incurring their treatment because they have done something criminally wrong. From their point of view a condemnatory, punitive element is not erased. It may make *us* feel better to call the institution to which the offender is sent a "hospital" rather than a prison, but he will know that this is not completely the case as long as he is adult and alert. (Compare the situation of political dissidents who are sent to "mental institutions" in certain countries.) Talk of his incurring the treatment—and all the medical-sounding talk of treatment—is in fact misleading. The so-called treatment, however benign, is *imposed* on the offender; there is a one-sided use of coercion, in Kant's terms. It is not like the case of the sick person who voluntarily seeks out medical assistance. Humanitarian sentiments are better served if we realize that we are punishing the offender, whatever else we may be doing to him. We should not delude ourselves that punishment can be abolished, although reform of correctional practices is sorely needed.[23]

We cannot go into the details of Lady Wooton's interesting argument concerning responsibility, but one general comment can be made. Granted that there are difficulties in the criteria of responsibility and excuses, it seems to me socially dangerous to allow responsibility to wither away. A society that does not presume that most of its adult members are sane, intelligent, and in control of themselves in effect reduces them to second-class citizenship. It takes away their self-respect as moral agents—as persons who can in sincerity be told that they have done something wrong —and our respect for them as moral agents. Punishment with responsibility, for all its present faults, at least preserves this respect in theory.

---

[23] In C. S. Lewis' novel *That Hideous Strength* (New York: Collier Books, 1962), p. 43, a member of the nefarious National Institute of Co-ordinated Experiments is made to say: "It does make a difference how things are put. For instance, if it were even whispered that the N.I.C.E. wanted powers to experiment on criminals, you'd have all the old women of both sexes up in arms and yapping about humanity. Call it re-education of the mal-adjusted, and you have them all slobbering with delight that the brutal era of retributive punishment has at last come to an end."

CHAPTER SIX

Dispute Settling and Justice

In Aeschylus' trilogy *The Oresteia*, the replacement of blood vengeance by social institutions for the resolution of conflict is depicted as one of the great achievements of civilization. On a smaller scale it can be argued (see Chapter One) that the presence in a society of agencies for settling disputes between individuals is a point in favor of an assertion that a legal system exists in it. Dispute settling, in fact, provides a perspective for examining perennial problems of legal philosophy concerning the relationships among law, force, and justice. It has been maintained that law presupposes force, and also that law aims at the elimination of the use of force. It has been maintained, at one extreme, that justice is an absolute standard for evaluating laws, and at the other, that positive law and justice are identical. The following discussion is intended to exhibit some of the ramifications of these issues when seen from the perspective of dispute settling. But we shall not be concerned so much with expounding and criticizing theories as with an independent exploration.

Our first task is to examine the activity of dispute settling. In effect, we will attempt to supply a partial answer to a series of questions posed by the legal realist Karl N. Llewellyn. "What," he asked, "is a court? Why is a court? How much of what we know as 'court' is accidental, historically conditioned—how much is essential to the job?"[1] However, the institutions we formally know as courts are not the only ones that undertake the settling of disputes. There is, rather, a variety of dispute-settling processes engaged in by various kinds of bodies, public and private, formal and informal. These processes, which resemble each other in significant respects, might be called *jural-like* forms of dispute settling. I shall describe three main jural-like forms, and then consider whether all of them should be viewed as "legal" types. This issue bears upon the question of the existence of law in primitive communities and on the relationship between law and force.

Our second topic is the role of justice in jural-like dispute settling. We shall here be concerned with *procedural* rather than substantive justice. "Justice," goes the old adage, "should not only be done, it should be seen to be done." This involves *fairness* in conducting the dispute-settling process, in hearing a dispute and in bringing it to a resolution. It is possible for such a process to be conducted fairly and yet have an unjust outcome—for example, when an unjust law determines the judge's decision. But the importance of fairness in procedure is more than merely to give the appearance of justice.

About procedural justice I shall try to show, or at least make plausible, two things: first, that adherence to standards of fairness promotes the *settlement* of disputes rather than merely bringing them to an end; and second, that standards of procedural fairness are to some extent *context dependent*—that is, dependent on the kind of dispute settling taking place. This second point should not be too surprising, because each of the jural-like forms derives its special characteristics from the kind of settlement it aims at. The question of the role of procedural justice in dispute settling is the analogue of the problem of whether the existence of law (or lawmaking) presupposes satisfaction of certain moral requirements—the controversy between legal positivists and natural law theorists. Our second topic, then, is concerned with whether the demand for adherence to standards of fairness can be said to be based on the character of the activity of jural-like dispute settling itself.

As a way of foreshadowing my later discussion, it is here worth noting that many recent writers hold that justice in the administration of laws merely consists in applying the laws "correctly"; i.e., in accordance with the categories specified within the laws themselves. It would then be pleonastic to speak of the just administration of laws. But this view suffers from decided limitations within the sphere of dispute settling. First, a dispute may be settled without any application of substantive law; it may

---

[1] *Jurisprudence* (Chicago: University of Chicago Press, 1962), p. 374. Our inquiry is limited to courts as mechanisms for settling disputes between individuals. We shall not consider the role of juries in this process, nor shall we be discussing criminal trials.

be settled in a manner that is neither *against* a law nor *in accordance with* a law. Procedural justice, however, still has a role to play in such cases. Second, just as there can be dispute settling without reference to rules of law, so also it seems that standards of procedural fairness cannot be reduced to explicit rules or, at least, to rules that do not already employ the vocabulary of justice—e.g., "neutral," "impartial," "unbiased," "fair notice," etc.

JURAL-LIKE
DISPUTE SETTLING

We may now turn to a general characterization of jural-like dispute settling. This, in effect, is a "construction" of a general simplified conception out of certain types of dispute settling that resemble one another in some important respects. Perhaps it will be useful to begin with what jural-like dispute settling is *not*. Although jural-like dispute settling may serve the function of the forestalling or managing of conflict, it is not the forestalling of conflict by legislation which establishes common rules of conduct or the management of conflict by social programs. In World War II almost every nation hit upon a way of controlling conflict among the members of submarine crews—unlimited access to food. This is not the sort of thing I have in mind.

Jural-like dispute settling involves (1) a dispute settler, a particular *third party* (who may be more than one individual) who "stands between" (2) *particular disputants* and settles, or attempts to settle, (3) *their particular dispute*. There must be (4) some kind of *hearing* of the dispute, the presentation to the third party of each disputant's side of the controversy. And (5) the materials so received must be *used* by the third party in arriving at the settlement. There is a sad tale of two farmers disputing the ownership of a bean patch. They appeared before the Emir, who summarily ordered that the farmers be decapitated and took the land for himself. Now the Emir brought the matter to an end, but he did not settle the *farmers'* dispute. He did not even hear it. Jural-like dispute settling requires a setting of "persuasive conflict," as we may call it, and the use of its materials by the third party.[2] The Emir did not engage in the activity of "courting," to use a Llewellynism.

From this we see that jural-like dispute settling, which always involves a third party, must be distinguished from the resolution of conflict through bilateral negotiation or bargaining. Of course, if the parties should agree to settle their dispute by tossing a coin, we would have an analogy to jural-like dispute settling. But it would be only an analogy,

[2] The term comes from Thomas Nixon Carver, *Essays on Social Justice* (Cambridge: Harvard University Press, 1915), p. 85. Carver distinguishes five chief forms of conflict: militant, gambling, persuasive, economic, and recreational.

for although there is something like a third party, the element of persuasive conflict would be absent.

We also see that jural-like dispute settling should be distinguished from "good offices." In good offices, diplomacy may be used by a third party to bring warring nations to direct negotiations or to agree on a method for the pacific settlement of their conflict. Good offices are designed to enable the contending of the parties to be carried on through *verbal* means. Militant conflict is thus transformed into persuasive conflict. Whenever there is a tendency toward persuasive conflict and the emergence of a third party there will be an analogy to jural-like dispute settling. Nevertheless, good offices do not quite fill the bill, for the third party is not strictly a dispute settler. He provides an environment for negotiations, and he carries and interprets communications between the parties. He does not, as the dispute settler does, *use* the materials of the persuasive conflict in order to effect a settlement. The process of good offices can easily break down if one of the disputants perceives the third party as taking on a more mediational role, for this could be viewed as a violation of the kind of *neutrality* expected in good offices. Neutrality, of course, is also expected of a dispute settler. It is one of the main elements of fairness. But this poses one of the most difficult problems in the design of dispute-settling institutions—how to harmonize neutrality with the necessity of securing and using the materials that are the basis for settling a dispute. We shall discuss this problem later.

The example of good offices should not be taken to suggest that persuasive conflict is always preceded by militant conflict. The persuasive conflict which takes place in the presence of the dispute settler, the presentation of the sides of the dispute, is an offshoot of an antecedent conflict. But this can be a conflict of desires, of interests, of claims, of demands, of rights, or simply an inability to "get along." Conflict on the normative level may have an underlying basis in disagreement over questions of fact, and the third party, in certain kinds of dispute settling, will have to decide factual issues. The antecedent conflict may, but need not, result in militant conflict before it is expressed in verbal form. An important function of the institution of jural-like methods of dispute settling is the forestalling of militant conflict and "self-help" (hence the image of the third party standing between the disputants). It is possible to design jural-like methods that serve the wider interests of justice, but it is doubtful that militant conflict often serves this end.

Persuasive conflict and the use of its materials—two essentials of jural-like dispute settlement—are not uniform phenomena, however. Dispute settling varies in the kind of use to which the materials are put, which depends on the kind of dispute settling in which the third party is engaged. Though all forms of dispute settling are alike in that they involve a hearing and a use of its materials, these common characteristics are not manifested in the same way in all the forms. We shall return to this point shortly.

First, however, a few general remarks remain to be made about the *settlement* of disputes. We may approach this topic by considering a quotation from Sir William Markby, a nineteenth-century British jurist. Although Markby speaks about a judge, he can be construed as putting forward a general theory of jural-like dispute settling and as answering Llewellyn's question about what is essential to a court. Markby writes:

All that the judge absolutely requires is authority to settle all disputes which come before him. . . . A tribunal without law, though scarcely within our experience, is not a contradiction.[3]

Now I am in perfect agreement with the view that a dispute might be resolved in the absence of any substantive law governing the issues between the parties. The availability to the third party, Markby's judge, of pre-existent laws typifies only a subclass of a particular variety of jural-like dispute settling. My objection to Markby concerns the first part of the quotation.

Markby apparently holds that it is a condition of jural-like dispute settling, and its only condition, that the third party should have authority to issue a *binding decision* in the case before him. (We may assume a setting of persuasive conflict.) And he seems to identify the *settlement* with the binding decision that is issued. But bringing a dispute to an end by a simple fiat, binding as it may be, is not a guarantee that it has been settled. The Emir, in our tale of the two farmers, did *not* settle the farmers' dispute. Whether or not a decision of this kind settles a dispute depends, first of all, on its logical relationship to the terms or subject of the dispute. I shall later try to show how adherence to standards of procedural fairness promotes genuine settlement.

Secondly, moreover, we should bear in mind that the persuasive conflict in the presence of the third party is an offshoot of an antecedent conflict. Whether a binding decision settles a dispute or not depends also on the relationship it is supposed to have to the original conflict. If, for example, the antecedent conflict is comprised in part of conflicting attitudes between the parties—hard feelings—it is not at all obvious that a binding decision will resolve them. It might even exacerbate them. Similarly, a binding decision might leave conflicting interests in their original state of opposition. When is a dispute to be considered settled? Is it at the point at which the decision is made? If the terms of a decision are not carried out, if the decision is not actually enforced, has the controversy

3 *Elements of Law*, 6th ed. (Oxford: Oxford University Press, 1905), sec. 201.

been settled? The answers depend on what we mean by "settling a dispute." Markby's meaning is not the only one. Dispute-settling processes may have a variety of *aims* and, therefore, different forms of jural-like dispute settling are possible and various functions may be served by a third party in his capacity as a dispute settler.

Now it might be said that what Markby means by "settling a dispute" is an authoritative or binding decision as to which party is right and which is wrong, a decision as to whose contentions are in some sense justified and whose not. And it might further be argued that this is the only kind of jural-like dispute settling that ought to be regarded as "legal." Let us defer this issue until after we have looked at some of the forms.

We shall consider three chief forms of dispute settling: (1) *adjudication,* (2) *conciliation,* and (3) *therapeutic integration.* (These terms are used in many ways in the literature. What I intend by them will become clear in the sequel.) All of these occur in modern societies. Civil litigation, commercial arbitration, and (labor) grievance arbitration provide examples of the first. Mediation of industrial disputes provides examples of the second. And certain kinds of family counseling provide examples of the third. I shall describe these forms in rather "idealized" terms, without examining the subforms and mixed forms that may be closer to actual practice.[4]

ADJUDICATION   This is the only one of the three in which the third party "decides" the dispute before him—that is, makes a determination as to who is in the right and who is in the wrong. This determination can involve deciding questions of fact, if a disagreement over facts is at the basis of the dispute, and it can also involve deciding questions of law or other normative issues. The settlement itself consists in an *award* to the winning party, which is intended as a *final* resolution of the dispute. The award also has the character of a binding decision. It is, so to speak, the "content" of such a decision. The source of the adjudicator's authority to make an award of this kind may derive from the State, as in civil litigation, or from a private agreement of the parties, as is usual in commercial arbitration. Clearly, in this type

---

[4] See Fleming James, *Civil Procedure* (Boston: Little, Brown and Company, 1965); R. W. Fleming, *The Labor Arbitration Process* (Urbana: University of Illinois Press, 1965); Merton C. Bernstein, *Private Dispute Settlement* (New York: Free Press, 1968); Bernard L. Greene, ed., *The Psychotherapies of Marital Disharmony* (New York: Free Press, 1965); Jay Haley and Lynn Hoffman, *Techniques of Family Therapy* (New York: Basic Books, 1968).

of dispute settling—because a binding decision is involved—there is special need for *procedural safeguards* to insure the fairness of the process, although the parties naturally have a greater freedom to set the procedures when it is conducted under private auspices.

The aim of adjudication, then, is the final settlement of disputes by the kind of award just described, and this appears possible only when certain conditions are met. There must, first, be "joinder of issue." For the dispute between the parties to be decided, they must meet head on, with one side denying what the other claims. If, for example, Jones asks me to give $100 to charity and I simply refuse, although there is some kind of conflict between us, we have not yet joined issue in the required sense. But if Jones claims that I owe him $100 and I deny it, we have joined issue. We can then each present our arguments (the factual, legal, or other normative grounds of our contentions) to the third party, and he can decide, on the weight of the arguments, whose position is justified. The materials of the persuasive conflict function as premises for drawing such a conclusion, which in turn is the basis of the award.

A second condition for the occurrence of adjudicatory settlement is that the conflict must be of a kind that can be settled by making an award. Leaving aside the question as to the senses in which the adjudicator's act of "making an award" can be binding (legally, morally, or otherwise), the award that Jones, for example, is in effect claiming must be within the power of the third party to grant. The binding decision that expresses the making of the award is something like a *command,* a directive, and it seems that not everything can be commanded. I can be told to *do* something for, or *give* something to, Jones, but I cannot be flatly commanded to love him. (I can, however, be commanded to act in a loving manner and to try to develop loving dispositions.) Adjudication is possible only for conflicts that can be settled by feasible awards.

Last, let us consider the finality of the settlement. As mentioned earlier, the persuasive conflict that takes place in the presence of the third party is an offshoot of an antecedent conflict. There is no guarantee, however, that his binding decision, which is supposed to stamp "finis" to the controversy, will in fact settle the original conflict. The antecedent conflict of interests, for example, may partly remain in its original unresolved state after the binding decision is issued. (In cases of litigation between members of a family, it frequently happens that the original conflict is actually exacerbated.) We are guaranteed finality of settlement only for the dispute that is ultimately framed in the persuasive conflict. For the purpose of adjudicatory dispute settling, the persuasive conflict must be conceived as *superseding* the antecedent conflict. This does not hold for the other forms.

CONCILIATION   In the second kind of jural-like dispute settling, the
                                  aim is to achieve settlement of disputes by an
adjustment or *compromise* between the claims, demands, or interests of
the parties. It is not the job of the third party to decide the dispute and
make an award—in effect, impose a settlement—but rather to bring the
parties to an arrangement that both willingly, though perhaps grudgingly,
accept.[5] The terms of the settlement may be accepted by them as a final
resolution or as a temporary stopgap. Given that the task is securing the
agreement of the parties, it might be thought that how this is done is
immaterial (e.g., by unfairly tricking one of the sides) and that it is therefore unnecessary for the dispute settler to maintain a stance of neutrality.
But aside from the consideration that adherence to standards of procedural justice promotes genuine settlement, experience shows that con-
ciliational processes break down if one party has reason to suspect the
dispute settler of partiality. And even if acceptance of the terms is secured,
the aggrieved party might well renege. Individuals in conflict submit
their dispute to a third party because they are unable to resolve it through
bilateral negotiation, and mutuality of confidence in his neutrality is
generally a requisite of a successful outcome. This is especially true of
conciliation, which usually is a voluntary affair from the start.

Because the third party is not called upon to decide the dispute that
he hears, joinder of issue in a strict sense is not a condition of the conciliation process. Of course, there must be some kind of conflict between
the parties: one wants to practice on his trumpet and the other wants
to conduct a delicate experiment; labor demands a one-dollar increase
in hourly wage and management offers only fifty cents. The positions here
are in some way "incompatible"—otherwise there is no dispute to settle.
Analysis of this notion of "incompatibility" is beyond the limits of this
chapter.

Just as the conciliator does not decide the dispute, he also does
not decide between the arguments (factual or normative) that the sides
present to support their claims or demands. The conciliator's use of the
materials of the persuasive conflict therefore differs in important respects
from the adjudicator's. He does not weigh the arguments in order
primarily to decide who is right or whose demands are justified. Rather,
the arguments give him an understanding of the complexities of the conflict and a sense of the weight that the *sides* assign to their claims and
counterclaims, of what interests are at stake and what significance is
attached to them, of what is "negotiable" and what is not. He learns what
common interests could supply a basis for a settlement, and thus can
formulate and present *proposals* to this end.

[5] For a stimulating discussion, see Lon L. Fuller, "Mediation—Its Forms and Limits,"
Southern California Law Rev., 44 (1971), 305–39.

When a dispute is settled by conciliation it often happens that the parties will have to compromise over what each feels he is legally or morally entitled to. Resolution is unlikely as long as a party "stands on his rights" or sticks to a demand "on principle." The conciliator has the job of "de-ideologizing" the conflict, and will try to get the parties to focus on the broader interests that are at stake. One of his functions is that of bringing rational considerations into the discussion, and he must tactfully use his own persuasive powers to overcome hostility and deep-seated needs to assert one's superiority. Plainly, conciliation requires special skills over and above the ability to "run a court." Although we expect adherence to standards of fairness, the conciliatory process is naturally also characterized by a greater flexibility and informality than we are accustomed to in civil litigation.

We may now introduce an important problem in the philosophy of dispute settling. It has to do with the design of institutions. Is there some kind of fit between types of conflict and forms of jural-like dispute settling? Are certain forms appropriate to certain kinds of social context? Conciliation, it seems, has special significance for circumstances in which the parties stand in long-term relationships that would be impaired by the loser-lose-all variety of adjudicatory award. Conciliation, again, is the prevailing form of dispute settling in so-called primitive societies. One usual—and seemingly circular—explanation of this is that they are jurally underdeveloped and have not evolved to the point of dispute settling by adjudication. But the superiority of adjudication is hardly obvious for closely knit groups. A fascinating case is presented by the African Barotse. The Barotse kuta (court) has authority to adjudicate disputes, but an interesting turn of events occurs when it is suddenly discovered that the parties are near relatives. The kuta will then veer toward the more informal techniques of conciliation. Max Gluckman, a legal anthropologist, writes: "It is clear that were the demands of some British officers, that the kuta should follow English legal procedure, to be successful, the kuta would be prevented from fulfilling one of its main functions —the settlement of disputes arising out of the multiplex relations which are still basic in tribal life." [6]

THERAPEUTIC INTEGRATION

We have, of course, only touched the surface in the above accounts of adjudication and conciliation. Because of its fantastic intricacy, we will have to be even sketchier in discussing therapeutic integration. And because numerous differences in theory and style obtain among its practitioners,

[6] *The Judicial Process among the Barotse of Northern Rhodesia* (Manchester: Manchester University Press, 1955), p. 81.

our account will have to be more "idealized." This form of dispute settling seems especially appropriate for conflicts arising out of personality differences and "psychic incompatibility," and particularly for individuals whose relationships are intimate and affective. It is useful for us to think of it in terms of its best example, *intensive family therapy*. Perhaps we can agree with Georg Simmel, who states:

Family conflict is a type of its own. Its cause, its sharpening, its spread to non-participants, its form as well as its reconciliation, are unique and not comparable to corresponding features of other conflicts, because the family quarrel proceeds on the basis of an organic unity which grows through a thousand inner and outer connections.[7]

Intensive family therapy should be distinguished from family therapies designed to enable the parties to "cope" with each other on a more or less temporary basis. These are closer to conciliation, and for all we know may be more effective. Family therapy of the intensive kind seeks to bring about deep *psychic change* through which the personalities are integrated and the inner *sources* of conflict removed. Obviously anything like strict joinder of issue is out of place here. Although the parties are, by hypothesis, in conflict, they may not be able to formulate what the conflict is or where it lies. The therapist must get at the roots of their troubles, and this he does through the persuasive conflict that takes place in his presence. Its materials are interpreted by him as *symptoms* of the underlying conflict. As in conciliation, the third party does not have the job of deciding between the claims and arguments of the parties, but one of the serious problems in the therapeutic process is that parties do often seek to win over the therapist to their side.

Therapeutic integration stands at an extreme opposite to an adjudicatory award: plainly it cannot be couched in a command to do or to give. (In conciliation, at least the *terms* of the settlement can usually be put this way.) The fact that a procedure for change (e.g., self-expression, correcting misunderstandings, or gaining insight into difficulties) is outlined to the parties does not mean that therapeutic change is necessarily brought about. This depends on the skill of the therapist, a skill that is exercised in terms of his psychotherapeutic theory and, it seems, a substantive notion of "health" or ideal of family life.

Another point of contrast with adjudication is that it would be highly misleading to view the persuasive conflict of the therapeutic process as superseding the antecedent conflict. Supersession, as a matter of plain fact, hardly occurs. The two conflicts are almost indistinguishable aspects of the same conflict. But there is, nevertheless, a significant difference between them—the persuasive conflict occurs in *the presence of a third*

[7] *Conflict*, trans. K. Wolff (Glencoe, Ill.: Free Press, 1955), p. 68.

party, and a *neutral* one at that. It is very pertinent that the literature on family therapy should so much emphasize the therapist's "use of himself," his "empathetic neutrality," and his capacity to "relate to the parties in an impartial, unbiased manner." Neutrality is as functionally vital here as in other kinds of jural-like dispute settling. I shall give this point further attention in the discussion of procedural fairness.

The result of our survey of three chief forms of jural-like dispute settling is, I think, that there is no simple and univocal answer to Llewellyn's question "What is a court?" (viewing courts in their capacity as dispute settlers). In each of the forms we have a third party and persuasive conflict. But there are differences in the kind of settlement aimed at, and consequently in the roles of the third party and in the functions of the persuasive conflict. Empirical study of actual practice would reveal many subtleties we have not considered. It is interesting to note, for example, that a commercial arbitrator will usually disqualify himself if the parties begin to speak of a compromise, because it might compromise his own position. Such a course will not generally be taken by a judge in the public courts. Why the difference? This question is commended to the reader for independent study.

LEGAL
DISPUTE SETTLING

We can now take up the issue we earlier deferred, whether or not all three forms should be regarded as "legal" kinds of dispute settling. According to the standard view, only adjudication, which is like what Markby had in mind, should be considered a "legal" type. Should we endorse this position?

The adjudication theory, as we may call it, has a definite attractiveness. By super-adding a binding decision to the other characteristics, we have a neat package that will appeal to those who see the law as something imposed from above or as imposing obligations willy-nilly. Moreover, "juralness" carries the connotation of officiality, and we can easily locate the official *jural act* in the decision which is binding on the parties. To the extent that adjudication occurs in a society, we can also say that jural agencies for settling disputes exist in it.

Despite all this I am hesitant to endorse the theory. Conciliation and therapeutic integration may well exist under the aegis of a legal system. A system could even show a preference for conciliation or therapeutic integration over adjudication. Maimonides, the medieval philosopher and jurist, compares the judge to a physician. Just as the expert physician uses diet or mild medicines before he resorts to drastic drugs, so will the good judge (a kind of social doctor) first seek to reconcile the parties rather than adjudicate their dispute. This is in fact official policy in many jurisdictions today. There are also governmental agencies for conciliating (mediating) industrial conflicts. In such cases it is true that the dispute settler does not act in a judicial capacity, if this refers to adjudication. But he would be engaging in a jural-like activity. I do not think that a society which, on the basis of a considered preference, officially provided only for conciliation or therapeutic integration, could be said to lack jural agencies for settling disputes between individuals. I might agree to reserve the appellation "legal" for adjudication, but only so long as the other forms are not thrown into a "nonjural" category (even when they are conducted under private auspices).

I referred earlier to the view that a society is jurally underdeveloped if it lacks institutionalized mechanisms for adjudication. The reason for this position is that it would be uncertain as to how conflict is going to be resolved when all else (e.g., bilateral negotiation, conciliation) has failed. I grant that such a society would be jurally deficient. But this should be balanced against the fact that in modern systems the public courts will not undertake to adjudicate every kind of dispute. For example, no court will agree to decide the controversy between Mr. and Mrs. Jones over where they should spend their summer holiday. Industrial disputes also contain plentiful examples. Suppose a new labor contract is being negotiated; the union demands a three-week vacation with pay, but management offers only two weeks. No court in the United States would at present undertake to adjudicate this issue. Such a controversy is said to be "nonjusticiable," for there is no applicable law under which it could be decided.[8] The parties will therefore have to find some other way of settling their dispute.

As to societies in which there are no established agencies for dispute settling, I think we should adopt a position of methodological tolerance. Conciliation is widely practiced in so-called primitive or jurally underdeveloped societies. It seems plausible to hold that there is a trend toward the existence of a "jural-like agency" for settling disputes when there is a general tendency to submit disputes to a relatively stable pool of conciliators. Such a circumstance can count in favor of an assertion that a legal system exists in a society. The existence of jural-like agencies and, perhaps, the existence of a legal system are matters of degree.

Before we conclude this part, a few words might be said about the rather complex subject of the relationship between law and force. The preceding discussion indicates, for one thing, that there is no straightforward and simple connection between at least two of the jural-like activities and force. They show the possibility of "law without sanctions."

---

[8] For a discussion of this concept, see G. Marshall, "Justiciability," in A. G. Guest, ed., *Oxford Essays in Jurisprudence* (Oxford: Oxford University Press, 1961), pp. 265–87.

Even if there is official pressure to submit disputes to conciliation or therapeutic integration, and even if the outcome of these processes should be made legally binding on the parties in some way, there obviously remain many phases in these processes for which any threat of force would only be a mistake. These processes will, in fact, lose their integrity as pressure increases to engage in them and as their voluntariness diminishes. Conciliation will become compulsory arbitration, a kind of adjudication. And therapy will become a manipulation or a remaking of personalities by nonjural-like methods. Given the rather limited sphere of conflict in which therapeutic integration is applicable, it is hard to think of its extension without conjuring up the images of the "brave new world" or 1984. (If there are residual doubts about the jural-like character of therapeutic integration—and I confess to having such doubts—it is partly because we do not understand how the therapeutic process really works.) Of course, nothing that I have said here should be taken as implying the feasibility or desirability of eliminating adjudication, particularly adjudication in accordance with laws.

PROCEDURAL JUSTICE

The second subject we have set for exploration in this chapter is *procedural justice*. Procedural justice governs, especially, the hearing of a dispute and also the way in which the settlement is arrived at, the third party's reception and use of the materials of the persuasive conflict. Although the demand for it is especially stringent in adjudication, we also expect fairness in the conducting of conciliation and therapeutic integration. Third-party neutrality, for example, which is a major aspect of fairness, is vital in all the forms. An examination of the functions and operations of procedural justice in dispute settling, therefore, provides an important focus of comparison and contrast, even if one holds that only adjudication is a "legal" type. We can deal with just a few facets here.

Does the need for fairness in procedure follow in some way from the very nature of the activity of jural-like dispute settling? This is our main question. If this is the case, a society that provided agencies for the settling of disputes between individuals would necessarily have to build procedural justice into the design of such institutions.

I think that this view has some initial plausibility when we consider that jural-like dispute settling involves the attempt to settle the *particular disputes of particular parties*. We would be hesitant to say that a system which provided "courts" in which the dispute settler was always fatally biased against one of the parties (e.g., if one of the disputants were always made the judge) had really provided jural procedures for settling disputes, let alone just procedures. Now, it seems clear that jural-like dispute settling will wither on the vine if parties in conflict have no confidence in the fairness of the proceedings. For if the contenders have any choice in the matter, they generally will not submit their dispute to a third party whose neutrality, for example, is suspect. But the view we are considering goes further than the question of confidence, important as that is. It suggests that the desire for institutions and methods in which we can have this kind of confidence is in part based upon something more fundamental—namely, a special kind of connection between jural-like dispute settling and procedural justice.

Unfortunately, there is no name for this connection. One might describe it by saying that the concept of "dispute settling" is parasitic on the concept of "fair dispute settling." Putting the connection in this way has the advantage of not making it self-contradictory to speak of corrupt dispute settlers or unfair trials. It does imply that we cannot understand what a trial or hearing is without the concept of a fair trial or hearing. It amuses us that the ancients determined guilt by examining the entrails of chickens. But, by analogy with the above, we can identify this as a "judicial," and not simply a magical, proceeding because the ancients believed that the relevant questions could be decided in this way *and* the determination of such questions is an element of a judicial proceeding.

Nevertheless, the above statement of the connection is somewhat obscure, and I prefer the formulation used in our earlier discussion; namely, that adherence to standards of fairness *promotes* the settlement of disputes. A few points should be noted about this. First, adherence to fairness does not guarantee that the outcome of a jural-like process will be fair by some substantive standard. It does not even guarantee that the outcome will in fact be a settlement of the parties' dispute. On the other hand, violation of fairness does not preclude the possibility of a genuine settlement, but such an eventuality would be more a matter of accident than design. Finally, adherence to fairness does increase the likelihood that the outcome is a genuine settlement, and *this* is not a matter of accident or of some purely contingent correlation between fairness and jural-like dispute settling, but rather a consequence of the nature of the activity. I shall try to show the plausibility of this thesis in the treatment of the standards of procedural justice.

JUSTICE AND EQUALITY   It is useful to begin by first setting procedural fairness within the context of generic notions of justice.[9] We shall not survey the immense literature dealing with justice as a virtue, justice in the practice of punishment,

[9] *Ethics* (2nd ed.), William Frankena, and *Social Philosophy*, Joel Feinberg (Englewood Cliffs, N.J.: Prentice-Hall, Inc., 1973) of this series, Chaps. 3 and 7 respectively.

justice in the distribution of goods (social justice), and justice in the exercise of public authority. Our interest here is limited to a few key ideas. It is worth noticing that the historically earliest demands for justice apparently were of a procedural variety, like the Biblical injunctions to judges "to hear the small as well as the great" (Deut. 1: 17), not to take bribes (Deut. 16: 19), etc. It seems, however, that procedural justice is a subordinate kind of justice. For there is little point in devising standards or rules of fair procedure unless following them results in just decisions and outcomes. If the substantive law is unjust, it does not seem to matter much whether the procedural rules are fair or not. Nevertheless, we should distinguish standards of fair procedure from the *ideal* of justice in terms of which the standards are elaborated. It may be that individuals have the same entitlement to justice in the hearing of their disputes as they do to be governed by substantively just laws. What we have, therefore, is a difficult problem in institutional design in which one entitlement must be weighed against the other. To what extent, for example, should one's claim to a fair hearing be overriden by the desire to reach a just resolution in a dispute? Can we formulate standards in which all these entitlements are given their due? Questions of this sort arise in the elaboration of procedural law, in which a multiplicity of ends, including the efficiency of the system, must be taken into account. What makes the problem of design so difficult is, I think, that adherence to standards of fairness *does* promote the settlement of disputes.

The prevailing tradition in philosophy relates the core sense of "justice" to the idea of *equality*. This goes back to Aristotle, who tells us that justice consists in treating equals equally and unequals unequally. Equality is the *formal* element in justice, and according to Alf Ross, it simply means that a society should have rules or laws and follow them.[10] This is inadequate, as Henry Sidgwick pointed out in his criticism of the proposition that the law itself is the standard of justice.[11] For we criticize laws and rules on grounds of justice. Nevertheless, the formal element is of real importance. It requires that laws be administered impartially, that like cases be treated alike. But more than this, it requires that action, especially that of public officials and others who exercise authority, should not be capricious or arbitrary, but based on principle. The exclusion of arbitrariness seems more fundamental to the concept of justice than equality alone. It encompasses the interrelated notions of rationality, objectivity, consistency, impartiality, and equality. In third-party dispute settling it also includes the notion of neutrality, which is especially related to objectivity, impartiality, and equality. Nonarbitrariness can be de-

[10] *On Law and Justice* (London: Stevens and Sons, Ltd., 1958), Chap. 12.

[11] *Methods of Ethics,* 7th ed. (London: Macmillan and Company, 1907), p. 265.

termined only by reference to the grounds, values, and ends on which claims are made, and in terms of which persons and cases are distinguished. These supply the *substantive* element in justice. Aristotle recognized the indispensability of this element when he said that justice consists in equality and inequality, but "which equality and which inequality this means is a political question" (*Politics*, 1282b 21). The ideal of justice is comprised of the formal and substantive elements. Further exploration of this would take us into the field of moral philosophy.

Although the formal element is a complex of notions, the relative significance of any component seems to depend on the context in which questions of justice arise. Thus, in the hearing stage of the dispute-settling process, equality is of special importance. Aristotle, according to whom the distribution of goods and honors should depend on merit, recognizes this in holding that it makes no difference whether a good man defrauds a bad or a bad man a good, the law should treat the parties as equals. This obviously applies not only to impartial application of a legal rule but also to the hearing of their case. But it is not enough for the dispute settler merely to treat the parties in an equal fashion. Standards and rules of fair procedure should be formulated so as to *equalize* and maintain the parity of the parties. A sense of this requirement finds expression even in trial by combat, as depicted on medieval manuscripts portraying a "trial" between a man and a woman. "The chances between such unequal adversaries were adjusted by placing the man up to the navel in a pit three feet wide, tying his hand behind his back, and arming him only with a club, while his fair opponent had the free use of her limbs and was furnished with a stone as large as the fist, or weighing from one to five pounds, fastened in a piece of stuff." [12] Equalizing the parties can in fact pose problems for the dispute settler, who is required to keep neutral. In a litigation in which one party is represented by a smart lawyer and the other by a dumb lawyer, it will be hard for the judge to equalize the parties without appearing to "play the part of an advocate."

Equalizing the parties, however, is insufficient. Treating persons equally badly is not necessarily giving them justice. A party should not only have an equal opportunity to state his side of the dispute but also a *fair* or *adequate* opportunity. This probably brings some consideration of substantive justice into the situation. The parties are *entitled* to this kind of opportunity because their rights or interests are in jeopardy. But this requirement seems also to connect with notions of rationality and objectivity. Arriving at a (substantively) just decision or outcome, especially (though not only) when questions of fact are in dispute, depends upon the dispute settler's having a true or reasonable estimate of the relevant

12 Henry C. Lea, *Superstition and Force*, 4th ed., rev. (Philadelphia: Lea and Bros., 1892), p. 153.

issues. Justice requires truth or reasonableness. (An alleged criminal has been unjustly convicted if we cannot truthfully or reasonably say that he committed the crime.) For this reason the parties should have a fair or adequate opportunity to present their sides, so that contentious issues will be clarified and the dispute settler will have a sufficient and objective basis for his decision, proposal, or action. This means, particularly in adjudication, the formulation of rules of evidence for the rational weighing of the materials presented in the persuasive conflict. The actual, physical weighing of the documents that Judge Bridlegoose, in Rabelais' *Gargantua and Pantagruel,* took pride in may have been better than the performance of the corrupt judges of his day, but it was obviously unsatisfactory. The securing of adequate and rational grounds for action, however, poses problems in institutional design. Torture is plainly an unacceptable device. But to what extent should the third party be permitted to conduct an independent inquiry into the details of the conflict? This leads to the debate over the relative merits of the Anglo-American adversary system and the so-called continental inquisitorial process. The question takes on a different color depending on the jural-like form about which it is raised, and is one of the things that suggests the context-dependence of standards of fair procedure.

**STANDARDS
OF PROCEDURAL
JUSTICE**

With the above in mind, let us now turn to the standards of procedural justice.[13] The listing that follows, which is not necessarily intended as complete, is primarily formulated in regard to *adjudication.* We shall not be able to discuss each item in detail, nor shall we be able to consider whether and how each might need to be qualified for other forms of dispute settling. For convenience, the list will be put under three headings:

Neutrality
1. "No man should be judge in his own cause."
2. The dispute settler should have no private interest in the outcome.
3. The dispute settler should not be biased in favor of or against a party.

Persuasive Conflict
4. Each party should be given fair notice of the proceedings.
5. The dispute settler should hear the argument and evidence of both sides.
6. The dispute settler should hear a party only in the presence of the other party.

[13] See Robert S. Summers, "Law, Adjudicative Processes, and Civil Justice," in G. Hughes, ed., *Law, Reason, and Justice* (New York: New York University Press, 1969), pp. 169–85; C. K. Allen, *Aspects of Justice* (London: Stevens and Sons, Ltd., 1958); F. E. Dowrick, *Justice According to the English Common Lawyers* (London: Butterworths, 1961).

7. Each party should be given a fair opportunity to respond to the arguments and evidence of the other party.

Settlement
8. The terms of the settlement should be supportable by reasons.
9. The reasons should refer to the arguments and evidence presented.

Many, perhaps all, of the above are contained in what English jurists call *natural justice.* They have been considered so fundamental that, despite the doctrine of parliamentary supremacy, some English judges have said that an act of Parliament against them would be void in itself.

Numbers 1, 5 and 9 seem to have a special status, for they, in a sense, define jural-like dispute settling. The first has also been construed to demand of a society, if it is to be a just society, that it provide mechanisms or agencies for the settling of disputes. (See the opening sentence of this chapter.) And obviously, these institutions ought to operate in a fair manner, giving the parties a sense of fair treatment. One reason is that fairness, I think, *promotes settlement* and the other is simply the matter of *confidence,* without which the institutions will not survive. The dispute settler, therefore, should be neutral as between the parties; he should be impartial and unbiased. Standard 2 helps to insure neutrality and maximize confidence.

So do the standards governing the persuasive conflict. They comprise, in a sense, the *operational* definition of neutrality—neutrality in practice. Suspicion of bias, and perhaps bias itself, can be overcome or kept within bounds if the dispute settler must hear both sides, and that in the presence of both parties. But adherence to these standards does more than help insure neutrality and equalize the parties. It raises the "litigation quality" of the whole process: disputed issues are brought out into the open and the scope and terms of the conflict receive clarification. Not only is the sense of fair treatment maximized, because a party will have some assurance that the dispute settler's actions will be based on material that the party has heard and to which he has had a chance to respond, thus mitigating the effects of "surprise," but also a more adequate and objective basis for action is achieved. We cannot here discuss procedural devices that would implement these standards.

We can see, I think, how these standards bring together various components of the concept of justice and how they tie in with third-party neutrality. They are, however, in need of qualification for the other forms of dispute settling. Although it would be quite improper for a judge in an adjudication to invite one of the parties for lunch to tell his side of the dispute in private, this would not be out of place in most conciliations. It is, in fact, not an uncommon practice in labor mediation. The explanation of this is plain. In adjudication the dispute settler *decides* the dispute, and in effect imposes the settlement; in conciliation the parties *agree* to the settlement. If the excluded party is satisfied with the dispute settler's proposal, he will accept it despite the private lunch. And if he is bothered by the private lunch, he can simply refuse to accept the proposal. Of course, the agreement of both parties must be secured, and hence the need for objectivity, impartiality, etc. Neutrality, here, is first of all openness and receptivity in a fashion that maintains parity and, secondly, objectivity and impartiality in explaining the position of one party to the other, in showing the reasonableness or unreasonableness of a demand, and in pointing the path to an agreement. The conciliator, it should be remembered, enters the conflict because the parties are unable to resolve it through bilateral negotiation.

A further explanation of this variation between adjudication and conciliation is that only in the former is there "joinder of issue" in a strict sense, so that the process is dominated by narrower notions of what is *relevant* to deciding the dispute. Each party will, therefore, be quite concerned about what material is presented to the adjudicator and what might influence his decision. Finally, there is the matter of substantive justice, to which conciliation has a more complex and problematic relation than adjudication. Procedural justice should serve the interests of substantive justice, and we have already considered some of the difficulties that lie in the way. In conciliation, however, it is not simply substantive justice which is at stake, if it is a stake at all, but a workable arrangement that the parties can "live with" and for which each has to compromise what he feels he is entitled to. Conciliation, therefore, is characterized by a greater flexibility, and this reflects back on the standards of fair procedure.

Therapeutic integration is an even more complicated story, and we cannot go into details on how it affects the standards of fairness. Interestingly, most family therapists and marriage counselors are quite cautious about seeing a party in private. They will do so only if there is pressing need, and will inform the party that their conversation will not be held in confidence if it reveals an issue that should be brought out into the open. The dispute settler must keep neutral, and not appear to "take sides." (It is striking how the literature on all the forms of jural-like dispute settling emphasizes this.) One reason why the question of standards of fairness in therapeutic integration is so difficult and elusive is that the persuasive conflict does not supersede the original conflict, so that the therapist is a *participant* in the family conflict. He is a participant who is not deciding a dispute or seeking an agreement, but a participant who is affecting human relationships through the therapeutic technique. But he is a participant of an odd kind—a neutral participant. He must be receptive to both sides, give each an opportunity to respond to the other, be objective, receive adequate information, and so on.

After the persuasive conflict we come, finally, to the settlement. The eighth standard of procedural justice tells us that the terms of the settlement (the adjudicatory decision, the conciliatory proposal, the therapeutic measures) should be based upon reasons, for justice excludes arbitrariness. And, according to the ninth standard, these reasons should refer back to the materials presented in the persuasive conflict. *How* they should make reference to the materials of the persuasive conflict raises questions about deliberative reasoning and also policy questions. In adjudication conducted within the framework of a legal system, the dispute settler's use of these materials is determined by the relevant law; and in therapeutic integration it is determined by psychotherapeutic theories and a concept of "health." A conciliation might also have to take into account wider economic factors. This standard, like the others, is context-dependent and its details need to be worked out.

In coming to the last group of standards we see the plausibility of the thesis that adherence to procedural fairness *promotes* the settlement of disputes rather than merely bringing them to an end. Jural-like dispute settling aims at settling the particular disputes of particular parties. Standards 8 and 9 work in cooperation, so to speak, with the previous standards. Aside from the important issue of confidence—and we have seen how complex the matters are that go into making for confidence—adherence to the standards of fair procedure, taken together, focuses the terms of the settlement on the parties' dispute. If dispute-settling processes should serve the cause of justice, they should also settle disputes. Settling the parties' dispute takes us back to neutrality, objectivity, equality, and impartiality in the hearing stage of the process. But all these considerations also support the contention that the need for fairness in procedure follows from the very nature of jural-like dispute settling. If this thesis is correct, it establishes for jural-like dispute settling an analogue of the natural law position.

This conclusion, however, should be taken as tentative. Our study has been exploratory. The philosophy of jural-like dispute settling is unfinished. Further inquiry may be commended to the reader.

FOR FURTHER READING

In addition to works referred to in the footnotes, the reader may also wish to consult the items listed below. For an annotated bibliography see R. W. M. Dias, *A Bibliography of Jurisprudence*. London: Butterworths, 1964.

ANTHOLOGIES, COLLECTIONS OF ESSAYS, AND BOOKS COVERING A VARIETY OF PROBLEMS IN LEGAL PHILOSOPHY

COHEN, MORRIS, and FELIX COHEN, eds., *Readings in Jurisprudence and Legal Philosophy*. New York: Prentice-Hall, 1951.

GINSBERG, MORRIS, *On Justice in Society*. Baltimore: Penguin Books, 1965.

HALL, JEROME, ed., *Readings in Jurisprudence*. New York: Bobbs-Merrill, 1938.

HUGHES, GRAHAM, ed., *Law, Reason, and Justice*. New York: New York University Press, 1969. Essays by contemporary writers.

KENT, EDWARD A., ed., *Law and Philosophy*. New York: Appleton-Century-Crofts, 1970. Contains bibliography.

OLAFSON, FREDERICK, A., ed., *Society, Law, and Morality*. Englewood Cliffs, N.J.: Prentice-Hall, Inc., 1961.

SUMMERS, ROBERT S., ed., *Essays in Legal Philosophy*. Oxford: Basil Blackwell, 1968. Essays by contemporary writers.

Many texts on jurisprudence, though legal in orientation, are also of philosophical interest; e.g., texts by Dias, Fitzgerald, Friedmann, Jolowicz, Paton, Patterson, and Pound's five-volume collection of his writings in the field.

INTRODUCTION: THE SCOPE OF LEGAL PHILOSOPHY

FRIEDRICH, CARL, *The Philosophy of Law in Historical Perspective*, 2nd ed. Chicago: University of Chicago Press, 1963.

HART, H. L. A., *The Concept of Law*, Chap. 1. Oxford: Clarendon Press, 1961.

———, "Philosophy of Law, Problems of," in P. Edwards, ed., *Encyclopedia of Philosophy*, VI, 264–76. New York: Free Press and Macmillan, 1967.

POUND, ROSCOE, *Introduction to the Philosophy of Law.* New Haven: Yale University Press, 1922.

CHAPTER 1   THE NATURE OF LAW: PROBLEMS

BARKUN, MICHAEL, ed., *Law and the Social System.* New York: Lieber-Atherton, 1973.

HALL, JEROME, *Foundations of Jurisprudence.* Indianapolis: Bobbs-Merrill, 1973.

HART, H. L. A., "Definition and Theory in Jurisprudence," *Law Quarterly Rev.,* 70 (1954), 37–60.

KANTOROWICZ, HERMANN, *The Definition of Law.* Cambridge: Cambridge University Press, 1958.

LLOYD, DENNIS, *The Idea of Law.* Baltimore: Penguin Books, 1964.

RAZ, JOSEPH, *The Concept of a Legal System.* Oxford: Clarendon Press, 1970.

ROSS, ALF, *Directives and Norms.* London: Routledge and Kegan Paul, 1968.

VON WRIGHT, GEORG H., *Norm and Action.* New York: Humanities Press, 1963.

CHAPTER 2   THE NATURE OF LAW: THEORIES

CAIRNS, HUNTINGTON, *Legal Philosophy from Plato to Hegel.* Baltimore: Johns Hopkins Press, 1949.

GOLDING, M. P., ed., *The Nature of Law.* New York: Random House, 1966. Includes selections from writers discussed in this chapter.

LYONS, DAVID, *In the Interest of the Governed.* Oxford: Clarendon Press, 1973. A study of Bentham.

MORRIS, CLARENCE, ed., *The Great Legal Philosophers.* Philadelphia, University of Pennsylvania Press, 1959.

O'CONNOR, D. J., *Aquinas and Natural Law.* New York: St. Martin's Press, 1968.

SUMMERS, ROBERT S., ed., *More Essays in Legal Philosophy.* Oxford: Basil Blackwell, 1971. Essays by various hands on Bentham, Pound, Kelsen, Fuller, and Hart.

CHAPTER 3   THE LIMITS OF LAW

CLOR, HARRY M., *Obscenity and Public Morality.* Chicago: University of Chicago Press, 1969.

LEISER, BURTON M., *Liberty, Justice, and Morals.* New York: The Macmillan Company, 1973.

MITCHELL, BASIL, *Law, Morality and Religion in a Secular Society.* London: Oxford University Press, 1967.

PENNOCK, J. ROLAND, and JOHN W. CHAPMAN, eds., *The Limits of Law*. New York: Lieber-Atherton, 1974. Volume XV in the Nomos series of the American Society for Political and Legal Philosophy.

RADCLIFF, PETER, ed., *Limits of Liberty*. Belmont, Calif.: Wadsworth Publishing Co., 1966. Discussions of Mill.

WASSERSTROM, RICHARD A., ed., *Morality and the Law*. Belmont, Calif.: Wadsworth Publishing Co., 1971.

CHAPTERS 4 AND 5   PUNISHMENT

BRANDT, RICHARD B., *Ethical Theory*, Chap. 19. Englewood Cliffs, N.J.: Prentice-Hall, 1959.

EWING, A. C., *The Morality of Punishment*. London: Kegan Paul, 1929.

EZORSKY, GERTRUDE, ed., *Philosophical Perspectives on Punishment*. Albany: State University of New York Press, 1972. Contains bibliography.

FITZGERALD, P. J., *Criminal Law and Punishment*. Oxford: Clarendon Press, 1962.

GERBER, RUDOLPH J., and PATRICK D. MCANANY, eds., *Contemporary Punishment*. Notre Dame: University of Notre Dame Press, 1972.

GRUPP, STANLEY E., ed., *Theories of Punishment*. Bloomington: Indiana University Press, 1972.

HART, H. L. A., *Punishment and Responsibility*. Oxford: Clarendon Press, 1968. Important papers.

JACOBS, FRANCIS G., *Criminal Responsibility*. London: Weidenfield and Nicolson, 1971.

MOBERLY, WALTER, *The Ethics of Punishment*. London: Faber and Faber, 1968.

MORRIS, HERBERT, ed., *Freedom and Responsibility*. Stanford: Stanford University Press, 1961. Contains bibliography.

MORRIS, HERBERT, "Persons and Punishment," *The Monist*, 52 (1968), 475–501.

CHAPTER 6   DISPUTE SETTLING AND JUSTICE

AUBERT, VILHELM, ed., *Sociology of Law*. Baltimore: Penguin Books, 1969, Part III (Law and Conflict Resolution).

BARKUN, MICHAEL, *Law Without Sanctions*. New Haven: Yale University Press, 1968.

BIRD, OTTO A., *The Idea of Justice*. New York: Praeger, 1967.

DIESING, PAUL, *Reason in Society*, Chap. 4. Urbana: University of Illinois Press, 1962.

LUCAS, J. R., "On Processes for Resolving Disputes," in R. S. Summers, ed., *Essays in Legal Philosophy*, pp. 167–82. (Cited above.)

MICHAEL, JEROME, *The Elements of Legal Controversy*, Pt. 1. Brooklyn: Foundation Press, 1948.

————, "The Basic Rules of Pleading," *The Record of the Bar of the City of New York*, 5 (1950), 175–201.

PERELMAN, CH., *The Idea of Justice and the Problem of Argument*. New York: Humanities Press, 1963.

————, *Justice*. New York: Random House, 1967.

RAWLS, JOHN, *A Theory of Justice*. Cambridge: Belknap Press, 1971.

INDEX